Antique Lamp Buyer's Guide

Antique Lamp
Buyer's Guide

Identifying Late 19th and Early 20th Century American Lighting

Nadja Maril

Schiffer
Publishing Ltd

4880 Lower Valley Rd. Atglen, PA 19310 USA

Dedication

This book is dedicated to everyone who appreciates old lamps
and uses them in their home.

Library of Congress Cataloging-in-Publication Data

Maril, Nadja
    Antique lamp buyer's guide : identifying late 19th and early 20th century American lighting / Nadja Maril.
       p.   cm.
    ISBN: 0-7643-0427-5 (paperback)
    1. Lamps--Collectors and collecting--United States--Catalogs. 2. Lamps--United States--History--19th century--Catalogs. 3. Lamps--United States--History--20th century--Catalogs. I. Title.
    NK6196.M29   1998
    7491'.63--dc21   97-34938
                                               CIP

Designed by Bonnie M. Hensley

ISBN: 0-7643-0427-5
Printed in China
1 2 3 4

Published by Schiffer Publishing Ltd.
4880 Lower Valley Road
Atglen, PA 19310
Phone: (610) 593-1777; Fax: (610) 593-2002
E-mail: Schifferbk@aol.com
Please write for a free catalog.
This book may be purchased from the publisher.
Please include $3.95 for shipping.

Please try your bookstore first.
We are interested in hearing from authors
with book ideas on related subjects.

Contents

Preface and Acknowledgments

This book is written as a practical handbook, which I hope can be carried in a knapsack by people new to the lighting field who need a reference guide. Many readers have contacted me since *American Lighting 1840-1940* was first published in 1989, asking for practical advice on how to locate identifying markings and how to approach various types of restoration. They have also repeatedly asked, "What other books can I find on this subject?" Everyone, whether novice or advanced collector, wants more pictures and more catalogue material for reference.

All the photographs and original catalogue material in this book, with one or two exceptions, are different from those appearing in *American Lighting 1840-1940*. I have attempted to provide more illustrations of pieces not covered in my first book, rather than duplicate previous material. Thus you will find many more photographs of portable gas lamps and catalogue pictures of kerosene lamps, with fewer photographs of reverse painted lamps, Holophane shades, and early twentieth century desk lamps, all of which are extensively covered in my first book.

Readers in search of more information on lamps and lighting are urged to contact the Rushlight Club, as well as to read some of the texts about specific lamps and manufacturers listed in the section on Recommended Reading at the back of this book.

Several people were instrumental in helping this project come to fruition. Doug Palmer, of Brass Artcrafts in Annapolis, was kind enough to let me poke around his workshop and shared his knowledge of metals and their restoration, while Mary Ellen Heibel of Personal Property Appraisers explained to me the fine art of glass and porcelain repair.

I am very grateful for the help of Dan Mattausch, a devotee and researcher of original gas lighting who uses gas in his Washington D.C. home. Dan and his wife Nancy shared some of their collection to help illustrate the text. They also provided invaluable help in editing some of the material related to gas lighting and provided input to the price guide as well.

The majority of photographs were taken by Annapolis photographer Dick Bond, and I thank him for his excellent work. I would also like to thank the collectors and dealers who sent me photographs to use in this book or who allowed their pieces to be photographed.

Schiffer Publishing continues to be the publishing industry leader in making quality informative books on antiques and collectibles available to the public. I appreciate their support of this project and once again I enjoyed working with my editor, Donna Baker.

And last, but not least, I would like to thank my family for giving me the time, albeit reluctantly, to get this book written, particularly my husband Peter for helping to assemble and prepare the one hundred plus lamps for photographing.

Introduction

If you own an old lamp and you're wondering 1) what is it? 2) how was it originally used? 3) how can I make it look better? and 4) how much is it worth?...this book was written for you. It was not written for dealers who put together lamps from a multitude of parts to create the illusion of an antique they can sell for an inflated price, nor was it written for restorers who charge high fees for services you could easily do yourself.

There's an old saying in the antique business: you make your profit when you buy. If you pay a low price for something, it is easy to resell it for a profit. When you have finished reading this book and studying all the photographs and catalogue pictures, you should be able to buy lamps with confidence. But keep on studying and asking questions, because no one has all the answers. Part of my attraction to antiques is the joy of discovery and of learning about the past.

Each year hundreds of old lamp parts and pieces are thrown away as worthless junk by people who don't understand their purpose and their value. Meanwhile, lamp collectors are out combing flea markets, auction houses, and antique stores looking for these same items. You wouldn't throw away money, but each year many people do just that when they throw away old pieces of lighting. It is my hope that with the publication of this book more pieces of old lighting will be saved and preserved.

Definition of Descriptive Terms Used

For consistency, the descriptive terms used in this book strive to mirror those used by lighting catalogues and advertising from the era in which each particular lighting fixture was used. For example, although today we refer to lighting fixtures attached to the wall as sconces, they were originally known as brackets.

Great attention is given in the photo captions to identifying those portions of a lamp which may not be totally original. When the term "period shades" is used, it means the shades are from the same approximate time frame but are not necessarily original to the fixture or lamp on which they are being shown. When the description states "original period shades," it means that to the best of my knowledge the shades are original to this particular lamp.

If I know the shade to be a reproduction I will state so. It is unfortunate that a few lamp examples needed reproduction shades, but it is also important for the student of lighting to become well acquainted with the variety of reproductions available on the market.

In the interest of teaching as much as possible about the variety of finishes used on metal lighting fixtures and the various choices dealers and collectors face when considering restoration, I have tried to note whether a piece is in its original condition or has been polished or repatinated. A piece in its original condition that has greatly deteriorated is termed "in the rough." I have also noted whether a restored piece has been lacquered.

How to Use the Price Guide in This Book

I am always reluctant to write a price guide for fear that it will be misused. Please remember that the prices listed are intended only to be used as a guide. The prices shown only pertain to the exact lamp or lighting fixture pictured and described. The condition of the piece, its scarcity, whether it has been electrified, whether it has its original shades and original finish, and the individual buyer's desire to obtain a particular piece of lighting or component are all important factors in determining values. It is possible to find similar pieces of lighting for less than the lowest price in the range listed, as well as for more than the highest price listed.

Prices for the lamps and lighting fixtures pictured in this book show a range of prices for each item. Prices quoted are for the pieces as described in the photo captions. "Catalogue items" are priced based on general appearance and catalogue description.

Prices vary from one section of the country to another. The context in which a piece is sold, from a rural flea market to an elegant store in the expensive retail district of a city, can also affect the retail price of a lamp. Condition is very significant in pricing lighting. Is the piece functional? Does it need extensive refurbishing? Is the seller willing to stand behind the item being sold, or is it being sold to you "as is." These are all important factors. Often parts of a lamp have been changed or replaced, and the changes are not always apparent to the untrained eye. "Changed" lamps, described as such, are considerably less valuable and are priced accordingly in this guide for that reason.

It is not the intention of this guide to set prices. Dealer and auction prices vary greatly and are affected by demand as well as condition. Neither the Author nor the Publisher assumes responsibility for any losses that might be incurred as a result of consulting this guide.

Glossary of Terms

Argand burner
An oil or gas burner having a cylindrical flame supplied with air within as well as without to provide a maximum area of contact between flame and fuel.

Argand lamp
A lamp designed for use with an Argand oil burner, which usually has its fuel reservoir located horizontal to the burner.

Astral Lamp
An oil lamp with a ring shaped reservoir placed so that its shadow is not cast directly below the flame.

Bunsen burner
A type of gas burner in which a mixture of gas and air is burned at the top of a short metal tube, producing a very hot flame.

Candlepower
A unit for measuring light.

Canting device
A device which produces a tipping or sloping to one side.

Canopy
Circular shaped piece of metal used to hide the joining of a fixture to the ceiling or wall.

Chimney
Glass tube used to enclose the flame of an oil or gas lamp.

Colza oil
Rape or linseed oil.

Electrolier
A lighting device powered by electricity.

Font
A reservoir for containing the fuel in oil lamps.

Gasolier
A hanging fixture powered by gas.

Gas burner
A tube or tip, usually attached to a gas fixture, for regulating the flame of the gas consumed.

Gas key
On/off valve for regulating the flow of gas to the burner.

Gas Mantle
A mantle surrounding the flame of a gas jet which radiates light when heated.

"In the Rough"
The original condition of a lighting fixture when found in a rough unusable state.

Incandescent
Of or pertaining to a lamp, the light which is derived from incandescent material (material made luminous by heat) such as the filament in a crystal light bulb or the mantle in a Welsbach burner.

Kerosene
A mixture of hydrocarbons distilled from crude petroleum and used for burning in lamps; also called coal oil.

Lard
The semi-solid oil of hog's fat after rendering.

Patina
A coloration of metal achieved by age or by the application of various chemicals to the metal's surface.

Shade holder
Metal unit which, when attached near the light or burner portion of a lamp, has the purpose of holding a glass shade.

Student lamp
A kerosene reading lamp with a side fuel canister, which is easily adjustable for direction or distance of light rays.

Welsbach burner
A burner of the Bunsen type which also has a cotton-gauze mantle impregnated with thorium and cerium, so arranged that upon ignition of a mixture of gases, the mantle becomes incandescent.

Welsbach mantle
The mantle used in conjunction with the Welsbach burner. See definition above.

Wick
A band of loosely twisted or woven fibers, acting by capillary attraction to convey oil or other fuel for illumination to a flame.

Chapter One

Early Fluid Lamps

Several years ago a woman brought a lamp to me for an appraisal. It was a whale oil lamp, approximately 150 years old and made of amethyst glass. It would have been a very valuable lamp, but there was one major problem. About ten years earlier she had decided she wanted to use her lamp with electricity and had taken it to a "Lamp Repair Shop" for wiring. The "technician" had drilled a hole straight through the center of her lamp and mounted it on a wooden base so it would be just like a "regular electric lamp." To an antique collector, her lamp had become virtually worthless. What once may have been a six hundred dollar lamp was now worth less than one hundred dollars.

Don't let the same thing happen to you. Every year hundreds of lamps are ruined because people don't understand the importance of maintaining a lamp's original features. Many mistakes are made because folks don't understand how various lamps worked and functioned.

So, let's begin with the basics. If the lamp was fueled by oil it needs a container to hold the oil, called a font. The shape of the font is an important clue in telling you what type of fuel was used.

Whale Oil Lamps 1783-1859

One of the oldest types of lamps one may find still in use is the whale oil lamp. Although probably not still being used with whale oil, as originally designed, the whale oil lamp was easily converted to kerosene and then to electricity with the change of the burner and the addition of a socket and wiring. You can identify these lamps by the shape of their font (the reservoir used to contain the oil). The font is generally a long oval or slender inverted pear, as compared with the squat shaped fonts designed to hold kerosene.

Two whale oil style lamps. The lamp on the left is an original whale oil lamp made of flint glass in the bull's eye and drape pattern by the Boston and Sandwich Glass Company with the original pewter double wick burner, circa 1840, 9" x 4". $225-$350; the lamp on the right in amber glass is a 1920s reproduction made for electricity, as evidenced by its hollow body. 9 1/2" x 4". $35-$60. *Courtesy of Nadja Maril Historic Lighting.*

Whaling was a major source of income in the Northeast United States from 1789 to 1865. The growth of the whaling industry was due, in part, to the popularity of whale oil lamps.

First used towards the end of the eighteenth century, whale oil lamps began being widely produced in the early nineteenth century. The advantage of whale oil was that it gave excellent light and little or no smoke odor.

Two types of oil were used: whale oil, made from the blubber of the Greenland right whale, and sperm oil, from the cavity of the head of the Sperm whale. Sperm oil was considered superior because it burned longer; for the same reason, it was much more expensive. Due to its rarity and cost, sperm oil was reserved for use in public halls and on Naval vessels.

Whale oil burners consist of a single or double tube stuck through a cylindrical piece of cork or tin. The tube holds the wick in place and the oil is sucked through the bottom of the cylinder. You can easily identify a whale oil burner by these characteristics: the metal wick tubes projecting approximately 1/4" above the median disk, the small slot in the tube to adjust the wick, and the tubes extending below the disk into the font.

Cork burners on whale oil lamps are generally found with blown glass lamps and, very rarely, with metal lamps. Pewter burners could better withstand the wear and tear of constant removal in order to refill the font. Generally the font was glass and attached to either a glass, metal, or marble base.

The New England Glass Company in Cambridge, Massachusetts first began producing glass whale oil lamps in 1818. The Sandwich Glass Company in Sandwich, Massachusetts soon followed suit, producing closed glass lamps commencing in 1825. Both companies manufactured a variety of lamps in blown, molded designs. During the latter part of the 1820s, the mechanical production of pressed glass was developed. By the 1830s, the whale oil lamps manufactured consisted of blown fonts fused to pressed bases.

The first tall whale oil lamps with pressed feet were devised in the 1820s. Companies often used the same bases for whale oil lamps which they had originally designed as bases for bowls, glasses, sweet meat jars, castor bottles, and candlesticks.

Whale oil lamps produced after 1840 came in a variety of shapes and colors featuring the popular pressed patterns blown in a three section mold, such as sandwich star, waffle, waffle and thumb print, bell flower, horn of plenty, etc. Whale oil reservoirs are generally either a pear shape or a modified cylindrical

Three pewter double wick whale oil burners. $15-$25 each. *Courtesy of Nadja Maril Historic Lighting.*

Electrified whale oil lamp, circa 1850. Glass font, unusual figural stem of a woman's bust in cast metal with basalt finish, square marble base, brass fittings and cast brass decoration to hold ornamental crystals (replacements). 4 1/2" x 10 1/2". The acid etched and shallow cut 4" fitter shade, 6 3/4" in height, appears to be a replacement from the turn of the century. $275-$750. *Courtesy of Frank H. Gardiner, Forest City, Pennsylvania.*

shape with rounded shoulders. The fluid reservoir of a kerosene lamp looks like a flattened sphere. Whale oil glass lamps often feature lacy and frosted bases and chimneys which was the prevalent style during the earlier portion of the nineteenth century.

What proves confusing to collectors is that because most whale oil lamps were changed over for use with kerosene or electricity, their original burners were discarded. Thus you can not necessarily identify a whale oil lamp by its burner. Due to the scarcity of original whale oil burners, there are some collectors looking only to buy the original burners. Other early lighting enthusiasts focus on the different types and style of glass, as well as on the manufacturers.

Burning Fluid Lamps 1830-1859

Burning fluid lamps refers to lamps especially designed to burn a mixture of oil and other ingredients.

Lamps especially designed for use with burning fluids have much smaller and shallower fonts than those of a whale oil lamp. The reduction in the size of the oil bowls meant there was less space for heated gas to accumulate and subsequently explode. The shape of the font is very similar to that of a kerosene lamp.

The first burning fluid lamp was patented by Isiah Jennings in 1830. John Porter patented his fluid, "Porter's Original Patent Burning Fluid" in 1834. Porter's burning fluid was very popular because it produced a brilliant white light with very little smoke or odor. His secret was turpentine, which was distilled and purified several times and

Specially designed burner
for Burning Fluid Lamps

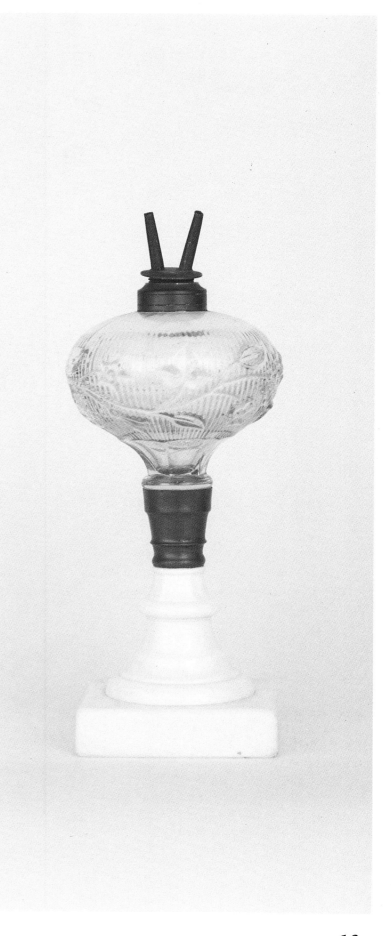

Burning Fluid lamp circa 1845. The clear pattern glass font is in the Bellflower pattern while the stem is brass and the pressed base is milk glass. Note the small rounded font. The splayed burner tubes are missing their small metal caps and chains, 10 1/2" x 4 1/2". $250-$350. *Courtesy of Ron Snyder Antiques, Annapolis, Maryland.*

then mixed with quicklime. The mixture, however, was very flammable.

Other burning fluid formulas used various concentrations of distilled turpentine, referred to as camphene. They also used camphene in addition to alcohol, naphtha, and benzene, while other lamps were used solely with camphene.

Porter's fluid was successfully marketed until 1859, but not without some hazardous results. Burning fluids were initially used in lamps designed for whale oil. The gas generated inside the glass font often exploded, causing major fires. Special burners were designed to minimize the danger of using burning fluids by keeping the heat generated by the flame as far away from the "burning fluid" as possible.

The tubes on burners designed for "burning fluid" are splayed and longer than those designed for whale oil. In order to keep gas from generating inside the font, the tubes do not project down into the oil reservoir. Small metal caps attached by chains were used to extinguish the flame and to prevent the evaporation of fluid when the lamp was not being used. Original burners for burning fluids are very rare because most people changed their lamps over for use with kerosene in the early 1860s and discarded the old burners.

Many of the same glass companies who made whale oil lamps also made lamps for burning fluid. Gradually the center for glass production moved from the Northeast to the Midwest. A good example of this was the New England Glass Company, which was located in Cambridge, Massachusetts and subsequently bought by Libbey. The Libbey Glass Company relocated to Toledo, Ohio and was tremendously successful between 1883 and 1940.

Colza Oil 1783-1859

Colza was a vegetable oil of high quality, which was used primarily in conjunction with the Argand burner. The Argand burner, invented in 1780 by Swiss chemist Aimee Argand, works on the principle of allowing air to flow both within the center of the flame and outside the burner. An Argand burner, when looking down on it, looks like two circles of metal with a wick sandwiched in between the two hollow tubes. Since more oxygen is supplied from inside and outside to the lighted wick, it provided a brighter flame.

The term **Argand lamp** describes a lamp which has an Argand designed fuel reservoir system in addition to the Argand burner. By 1783, Argand had devised an entire lamp in which the oil reservoir was located on the side and then fed across horizontally through an arm to the burner. The burner itself was fitted with a clear glass chimney. The side oil font was easy to fill and provided a steady supply of oil to the burner. The glass chimney prevented the oxygen fueling the flame from immediately escaping out the sides, thus creating a larger oxygen supply which resulted in a brighter flame.

Often designed to be used as a pair of lamps on a mantle, there are double Argand Lamps with a single central oil font as well as wall brackets and hanging fixtures. These were expensive lamps, primarily used by the upper class and thus made of fine materials. These materials included brass, silver-plate, and bronze, as well as marble and crystal prisms. They were not manufactured in the United States until approximately 1825. If colza was unavailable, Sperm whale oil was used to fuel these lighting devices.

Very few of these lamps remained intact. Their burners were removed and they were usually electrified during the early twentieth century. Therefore, you cannot identify them by their Argand burner, but you *can* look for a font to hold oil. If the lamp has no functional oil font, it is a copy of the general style, but designed for gas or electricity.

Engraving from 1844 *Webster's Encyclopaedia*, showing various Argand lamps and the construction of the Argand burner.

An **Astral lamp** also used colza and whale oil, and had an Argand burner. Also referred to as a Sinumbral lamp, an Astral can be recognized by its donut shaped font. The font is shaped like a ring and was designed to surround the wick. Unlike its earlier cousin, the Argand lamp, the Astral lamp's font is located in the center of the lamp. An Astral lamp was free from the shadow created by the font of an Argand lamp. The oil level was easier to maintain because it was centrally located.

While the burner has probably been removed, the font is usually still partially present below where an electric socket has been placed. The **Solar lamp**, discussed in the next section, is often confused with the Astral lamp because it also has a central font. However, the font on a solar lamp is always shaped like an inverted pear.

Lard 1783-1859

Colza oil and Sperm whale oil were very expensive. Lard, on the other hand, made from left over cooking grease, was available to everyone. However, lard solidified quickly and had to be reheated for use.

Many lard fueled lamps were made for the lower classes. These are utilitarian lamps made of tin, copper, or brass, simple in style. In order to keep lard liquid, a long wick tube was used to conduct the heat from the flame at the top of the burner down to the fuel supply. Additional mechanisms, such as pumps and canting devices, were used to bring the heat from the burner down to the lard. The majority of these innovations were patented, and have the date and company imprinted on the lamp.

One elegant lamp designed for use with lard was the **Solar lamp**. The solar lamp, popular in the 1840s, surrounded the burner with an oil font which looked like an inverted pear. The heat from the burner softened the lard. A metal "solar cap" with apertures forced more oxygen to the flame, and helped reduce smoke commonly produced when burning lower quality oil. The name, solar, compares the brilliance of the lamp to the sun.

Solar lamp signed "Cornelius & Co. Philadelphia July 24th, 1844, Patent April 1st 1843". Electrified brass and marble base with original chimney and shade, 5" x 22". $575-$1000. *Courtesy of Frank H. Gardiner, Forest City, Pennsylvania.*

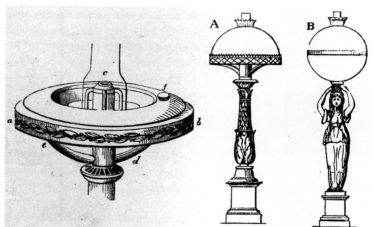

Engraving from 1844 *Webster's Encyclopaedia*, showing the reservoir and burner of an Astral or Sinumbral lamp.

Chapter Two

Lamps Designed for Use with Kerosene

Kerosene 1854-1930s

Most of the lamps for oil you will encounter in today's antique market were designed for use with kerosene. They come in all shapes and sizes. There were table lamps, floor lamps, wall brackets, hall fixtures, chandeliers, and desk lamps. The fonts to hold fuel were not all shaped the same. but generally, they are large, squat spheres. The exception is student lamps, which have a fuel reservoir shaped like a canister located on the side. Lamps for the previously described fuels in Chapter One were quickly converted for use with kerosene during the latter part of the nineteenth century, after the discovery of the first oil well in Titusville, Pennsylvania in 1859.

The first kerosene lamps date back to about 1850, but at that time kerosene was too expensive to be attractive to those already using other fuels. The availability of an inexpensive supply of kerosene changed people's attitudes. Within the first year of the opening of the Titusville well there were forty patents granted to inventors who were determined to make their burners, fonts, fuel cap covers, shade holders and various other mechanisms superior to those of their predecessors. Over a twenty year period, eighty new patents a year were granted to inventors of devices for kerosene lamps.

All these patents are wonderful for collectors because they provide an easy means to date and authenticate an American kerosene lamp.

Two basic types of burners were used with kerosene lamps. One was a modified version of an Argand burner, called a Rochester burner. It was named the Rochester burner because it was initially manufactured by the Rochester Burner Company of Rochester, New York. Invented by Henry E. Shaffer in 1888, it is also known as a central draft burner. The circular wick with air flowing inside and outside the flame was improved with spreaders or air diffusers.

The duplex burner worked on the principal that two wicks, side by side, create a stronger current of air. This enabled more oxygen to come into contact with the wicks.

A third type of burner, combining the attributes of both the Rochester burner and the duplex burner, was primarily used in small hand lamps and reading lamps. Less popular than the first two, it had a flat wick, but utilized the circular configuration of the Rochester burner. The air flow came from the sides of the burner.

While some companies only made burners, others made entire lamps which included shades and bases. The removable brass font was perfected in the 1880s by J.H. White and Associates. This innovation enabled a company specializing in porcelain or glass to create a beautiful base, and to purchase a complete unit which included oil font, burner, and shade holder from another company. The glass company might have created a matching shade for their base, while the porcelain company would have purchased a shade from a third company which specialized in glass shades.

The names of various companies may be found on the lamp base, burner, knob to raise the wick, shade holder, or oil font. There may be more than one name. A nineteenth century kerosene lamp usually has a name, and possibly a patent date somewhere, if the lamp is complete.

Three kerosene lamps, circa 1860-70, showing different size fonts. Left to right: A pattern glass clear font with etched vines and flowers attached to a milk glass base with an Eagle burner, 13 1/2" x 5" to the burner, $275-$375. Pattern glass font with copper wheel, engraved vine with grapes, marble base and brass embossed stem, burner marked "The Steel Mantle Light Co. Toledo Ohio U.S.A.", 12" x 4" to the burner, $300-$400. Cranberry glass inverted thumb print font with milk glass base, burner marked P & A Manufacturing Co, Waterbury Ct., 14" x 5", $375-$475. *Courtesy of Ron Snyder Antiques, Annapolis, Maryland.*

Kerosene lamp in the style of the Aesthetic movement, circa 1880. Metal portions of the base have been painted brown. Frosted pattern glass font with a hand painted floral design stem, Eagle burner, 14 1/2" x 4 1/2". $195-$275. *Courtesy of Ron Snyder Antiques, Annapolis, Maryland.*

Bradley and Hubbard Kerosene Banquet Lamp. B&H burner patented August 20, 1889, also with 1888 and 1890 dates. White metal and brass lamp with orange and green textured finish and removable brass font. The top column is ornamented with gilding and the footed base has wonderful open lattice work. Period frosted and clear shade with the Greek Key pattern has 4" fitter. Lamp is 24" x 8" to the burner. $425-$585. *Courtesy of Nadja Maril Historic Lighting.*

A close-up of the burners, shade holders, and fuel reservoirs from the Bradley and Hubbard banquet lamp and the Edward Miller Company extension lamp.

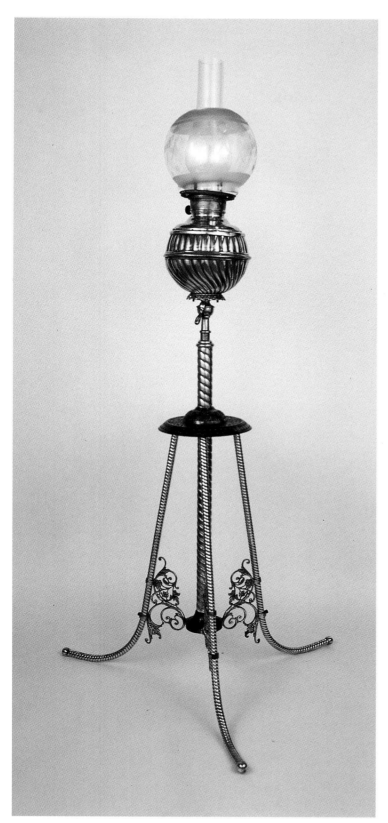

Edward Miller Company brass and base metal extension floor lamp, circa 1890. Polished, signed "E M" on burner and marked New Vestal E M & Co. on wick adjustment knob. 46" x 10" to the burner with 18" extension. Period clear and acid etched ball 4" fitter shade. $425-$525. *Courtesy of Nadja Maril Historic Lighting*.

Edward Miller Company brass and cast iron extension floor lamp, circa 1895. Improved knob to raise circular wick, "patented 1895" and marked "E M" on burner. 54" x 10" to the burner, with an 18" extension. Original period white opal glass 4" ball shade. $500-$600. *Courtesy of Nadja Maril Historic Lighting.*

The following illustrations are from the J.P. Marshall & Brothers catalogue of Kerosene Fixtures, Bronze Lamps, Etc., No. 27, John Street, Boston, 1876.

No. 094. Height, 10 in.   No. 095. Height, 10 in.   No. 0104. Height, 10 in.   No. 0106. Height, 10 inches.   No. 0113. Height, 9 in.   No. 0114. Height, 10 in.

Above: A selection of six kerosene table lamps from the 1876 J.P. Marshall Catalogue. $325-$425 each.
Below: A selection of Kerosene table lamps from the 1876 J.P Marshall Catalogue. Left to right: $550-$650, $325-$425, $425-$525, $425-$525, $400-$500.

No. 400. Fisher Girl. Height, 15 inches.   No. 250. Vase. Bronze Lamp.   No. 470. Boy and Rabbit. Height, 13 inches.   No. 480. Girl and Goose. Height, 13 inches.   No. 571. Height, 13 inches.

[40]

No. 830. **Fisherman.**
Height, 20½ inches.

No. 809. **Sculptor.**
Height, 18 inches.

No. 820. **Falconer.**
Height, 20½ inches.

22

Opposite page:
Three bronze figural kerosene table lamps from the 1876 J.P Marshall Catalogue. Left to right: $625-$725, $575-$675, $625-$725.

Right: Two cranberry glass peg lamps, circa 1860. These lamps were designed to fit into a candle holder so that kerosene could be used in place of candles. Marked F.T. Gale 129 Oxford Street Manufactured in Germany, 6" x 4". $175-$275 each. *Courtesy of Ron Snyder Antiques Annapolis, Maryland.*

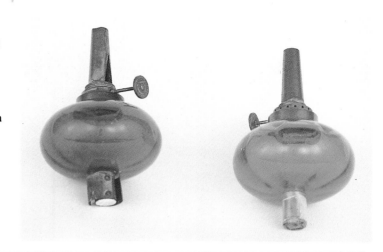

Below: Kerosene brass wall brackets, circa 1880, one complete and three incomplete. Complete bracket, 10" x 6 1/2", $200-$300; incomplete brackets, $10-$35. *Courtesy of Nadja Maril Historic Lighting.*

Kerosene cast iron wall brackets, circa 1880, 14" x 7". $485-$645 for the pair. *Courtesy of Janet Rothwell Smith.*

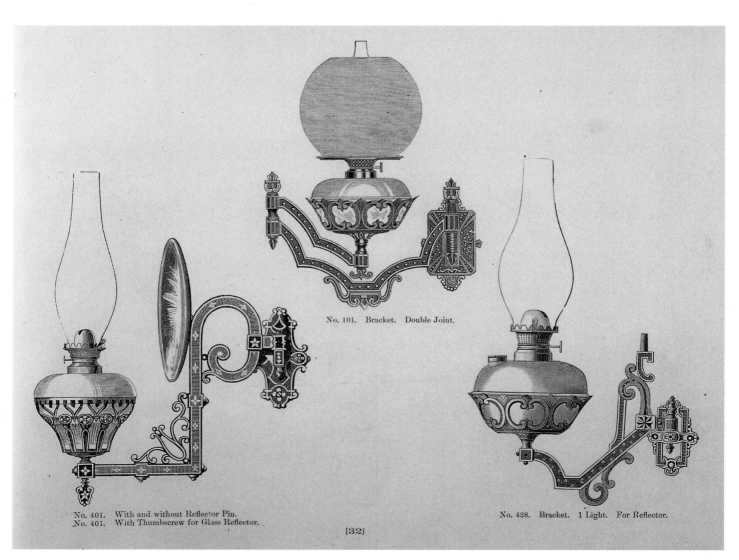

No. 401.   With and without Reflector Pin.
No. 401.   With Thumbscrew for Glass Reflector.

No. 101.   Bracket.   Double Joint.

No. 428.   Bracket.   1 Light.   For Reflector.

[32]

Three kerosene cast iron wall brackets from the 1876 J.P. Marshall Catalogue. Left to right: $225-$325, $300-$400, $200-$300.

24

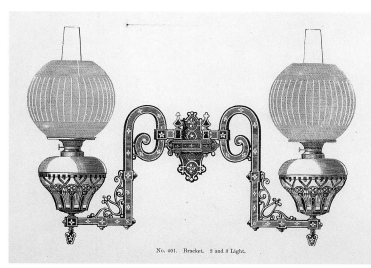

Double cast iron kerosene wall bracket from the 1876 J. P. Marshall Catalogue, $475-$575.

No. 401. Bracket. 2 and 3 Light.

Two kerosene hall lamps, circa 1880. Left: Cranberry glass, in unusual pear shape with decorative brass hardware, 20" x 9", $500-$600. Right: Acid etched canister shape shade decorated with swans, calling birds, and flowers. The brass has a satin finish. 30" x 7", $585-$685. *Courtesy of Nadja Maril Historic Lighting.*

The two hall lamps on the previous page with their chains lowered and shades raised, revealing the kerosene fonts sitting inside. In order to fill the lamp fonts with fuel the lamps would have been lowered for filling every few days, depending on how often they were used.

Two kerosene hall lamps, circa 1880, with original glass font and chimney. Left: Opalescent pink waffle glass with brass hardware, 21" x 8", $500-$600. Right: Ruby glass, brass fittings with gold finish, 25" x 8 1/2", $475-$575. *Courtesy of Nadja Maril Historic Lighting.*

Two kerosene hall lamps with round globes and original fonts and brass fittings, circa 1880. Left: Red satin glass with clear glass bull's eyes, 25" x 12", $500-$600. Right: Swirled dark cranberry glass, 26" x 10", $375-$475. *Courtesy of Nadja Maril Historic Lighting.*

No. 478½. Patent Pendant. Hinged Harp. Fount can be taken out without removing Shade.

Kerosene pendant from the 1876 J. P. Marshall Catalogue, $550-$650.

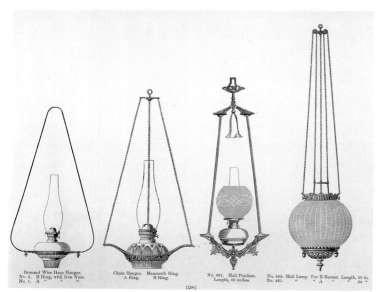

Kerosene hall fixtures from the 1876 J.P. Marshall Catalogue. Left to right: $110-$160, $125-$185, $275-$375, $300-$400.

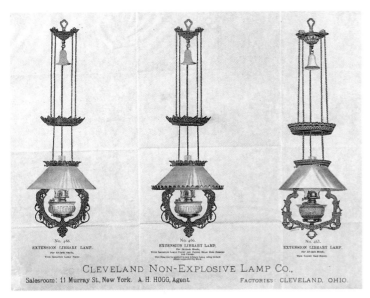

Cleveland Non-Explosive Lamp Co. Extension Library Lamp, circa 1875. $600-$700.

Two arm kerosene chandelier from the 1876 J.P. Marshall Catalogue, $750-$850.

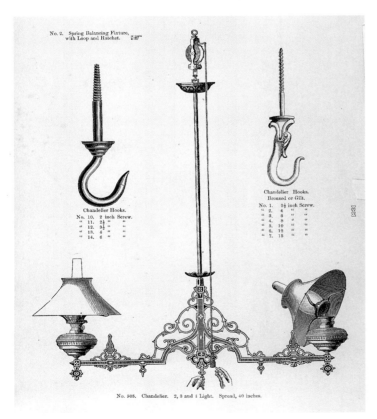

Two arm kerosene chandelier from the 1876 J.P. Marshall Catalogue, $785-$885.

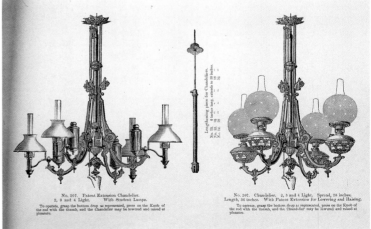

Two kerosene chandeliers from the 1876 J.P. Marshall Catalogue. Left: Four arm Student lamp chandelier, $1600-$2000. Right: Four light fixture, $1400-$1800.

Cleveland Non-Explosive Lamp Company Student Lamp, dated 1871 and marked "Argand" on the burner. Electrified in the 1950s, this lamp is otherwise "in the rough." The plated brass and brass surfaces have remnants of a gilded finish. 21" x 12" with a 5 1/2" diameter base. The 7" cased green glass melon shade is a reproduction. $275-$375. *Collection of Nadja Maril.*

Brass and base metal student lamp. Electrified in the 1920s, it has lost most of the original nickel plating and was probably polished and lacquered at the time of electrification. The bottom of the fuel canister is imprinted with "Close the valve after filling." 23" x 11", base diameter 5 1/2". Original period white opal glass shade. $475-$575. *Courtesy of Nadja Maril Historic Lighting.*

Edward Miller Company Student Lamp, embossed signature "The Miller Lamp," polished brass with brass plated pole and base, circa 1890. Embossed decoration features fan and leaf design. This lamp has a cased green glass reproduction replacement shade. 22" x 18" with a 6" diameter base, $725-$875. *Courtesy of Taylor Wells Antiques, Riverdale, Maryland.*

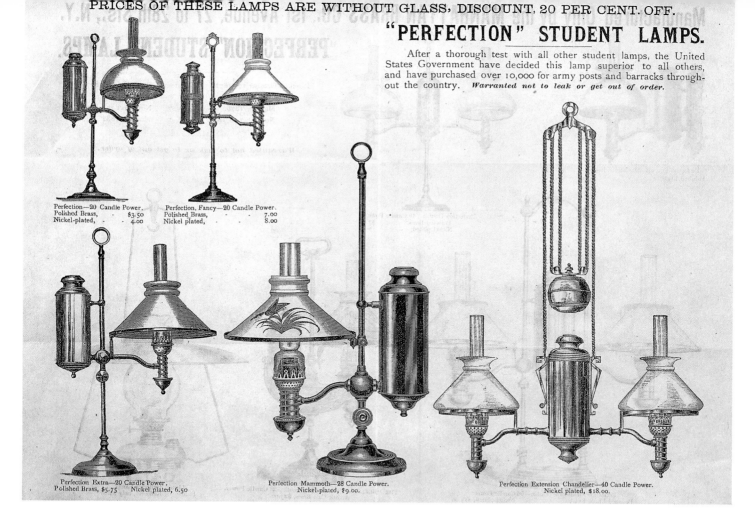

"PERFECTION" STUDENT LAMPS.

After a thorough test with all other student lamps, the United States Government have decided this lamp superior to all others, and have purchased over 10,000 for army posts and barracks throughout the country. *Warranted not to leak or get out of order.*

Perfection—20 Candle Power.
Polished Brass, - $3.50
Nickel-plated, - 4.00

Perfection, Fancy—20 Candle Power.
Polished Brass, - 7.00
Nickel plated, - 8.00

Perfection Extra—20 Candle Power.
Polished Brass, $5.75   Nickel plated, 6.50

Perfection Mammoth—28 Candle Power.
Nickel-plated, $9.00.

Perfection Extension Chandelier—40 Candle Power.
Nickel plated, $18.00.

"Perfection" Student Lamps 1882 sales brochure. Left to right: First three lamps, $475-$575, Perfection Mammoth $550-$650, Extension Chandelier $850-$1200.

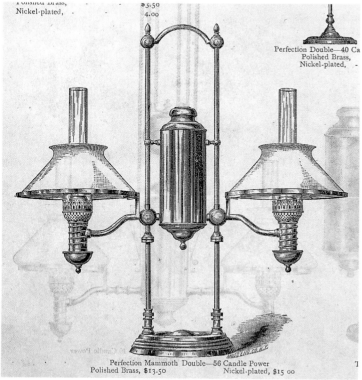

Perfection Double—40 Ca
Polished Brass,
Nickel-plated, -

Perfection Mammoth Double—56 Candle Power
Polished Brass, $13.50   Nickel-plated, $15 00

"Perfection" Double Student Lamp from 1882 sales brochure, $900-$1200.

THE GREAT
Wrigley Lamp

Height   Two Feet

Central Draft — 100 Candle Power
BEAUTIFULLY HAND PAINTED
SEE OTHER SIDE.

1895 Wrigley Lamp, given as a premium to General Stores with the sale of eight boxes of Wrigley chewing gum. $485-$585.

Electrified hand painted glass kerosene lamp with brass removable font, circa 1895, 9" x 24". $275-$450. *Courtesy of Frank H. Gardiner, Forest City, Pennsylvania.*

Kerosene night light, circa 1900. Swirled, clear pattern glass with burner marked "P & A Manufacturing Acorn," original chimney and pleated paper shade. 2 1/2" x 8 1/2", $48-125. *Courtesy of Janet Rothwell Smith.*

Three pressed glass kerosene lamps, circa 1915, all with burners by the P & A Manufacturing Co., Waterbury, Connecticut. The green glass and clear glass lamps both measure 10" x 5 1/2". The small hand lamp measures 3 1/2" x 4". $45-$75 each. *Courtesy of Taylor Wells Antiques, Riverdale, Maryland.*

Electrified double Angle lamp, brass and nickel plated with original patina, circa 1920; missing the pulley for raising and lowering the fixture. It does have its original clear glass inserts and white chimneys. 26" x 22", $575-$675. *Courtesy of Nadja Maril Historic Lighting.*

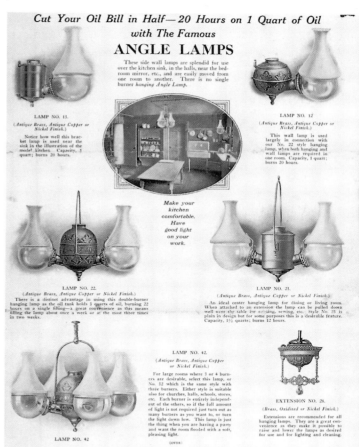

Top left and top right: Angle Manufacturing Company
1921 advertisement.

Angle Manufacturing Company 1921 table lamp,
$500-$600.

Gas Lamps 1817-1920

What identifies a lamp as having been used for gas if the original gas burner has been removed? Look for an interior tube to get the gas to the burner, and more importantly a way to turn the gas on and off.

Chandeliers and sconces (referred to as gasoliers and brackets during the era of gas use) received their gas supply directly from pipes located in the wall or ceiling. Since their pipe was attached to the gas source pipe, they did not have a large raised back plate or canopy which you would find in an electric fixture. When gas fixtures are electrified, the canopies are added to cover the electrical connections.

The gas key to turn the gas on and off came in different shapes. Some are highly decorated pieces of cast metal shaped like floral wreaths or open tassels while others are simple rings. The key worked the valve or cock by opening and closing the flow of gas through the gas pipe.

Most gas keys on gasoliers and brackets are located in the middle of the arm, although some (especially on crystal fixtures) are located right below the burner. This was a stylistic choice. On a table lamp, the gas key is often located at the base of the lamp, where the flexible tubing was joined to the lamp. The flexible tubing could be attached to various gas sources in the home, thus giving these lamps the term "portables."

The vast majority of gas fixtures found in the current antique marketplace date from after the Civil War.

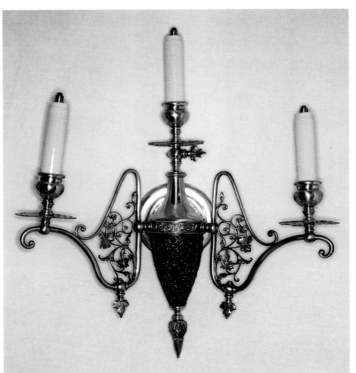

Three arm gas candle-style polished brass wall sconce, circa 1885, with original glass slips. 17" wide, 20" high, and 9 1/2" deep. $325-$750. *Collection of Erich Haesche.*

The easiest gas fixtures to find are from the late nineteenth century and early twentieth century. None of the gas fixtures illustrated in this book predate 1850.

The era of commercial gas production in the United States began with the opening of the first gas street lighting system installed in Baltimore, Maryland in 1817. Boston was lit by gas in 1822 and New York in 1827. Philadelphia chartered its own gas company in 1835. The operation of supplying gas to customers had become so highly developed that a meter was installed to measure the amount of gas used by each household in order to accurately charge for gas consumption.

Gas companies were located in large cities where the operation of producing gas from coal was cost effective. Other types of systems to produce gas were devised for use on country estates and in small towns.

Gas produced by the gas companies in cities was usually coal gas, or a combination of coal and water gas. Coal was heated, the hydrocarbons necessary for gas fuel were separated from unsavory components (such as ammonia and sulfur), and a gas which could be safely burned was produced. To make water gas, coke created from heating coal was doused with hot steam and the result was water gas.

Acetylene gas was a hydrocarbon gas generated by the interaction of calcium carbide and water. It was discovered by Edmund Darry in 1836 but not efficiently produced until 1892. It was widely available commercially by 1895 for use in rural areas. Despite some safety problems, 290 towns in the US were lit by acetylene gas by 1909.

Another type of gas had the trademark name Blau-gas. It was named after its inventor, German scientist Hermann Blau, and saw limited use after the turn of the century. A bottled liquefied gas, this product was advertised by the company as "an easy and economical solution of the problem of illuminating rural residences, factories, villages, towns, etc." Their companies were primarily located in New England and the Northern Midwest.

Blau-gas was described in sales literature as a mixture of hydro-carbon gases liquefied under high pressures and low temperatures. It was shipped in steel bottles, which were then placed in a small steel cabinet called the "expander box." In this cabinet, gas from the tanks was released into an expansion tank, and then piped through the house to be used for lighting, heating, and cooking.

Today gas customers use either natural gas, available in large cities, or propane (bottled gas). Unlike Blau-gas, propane needs no expander box or expansion tank.

Selection of portable gas lamps, pp. 37-46, courtesy of the Gaslight Collection of Dan and Nancy Mattausch. This rare group of lamps not only illustrates the evolution of technological advances in gas lighting during the second half of the nineteenth century, it also shows the changes in decorative styles. While most of these lamps are in gas burning condition, for clarity they are shown without their hoses.

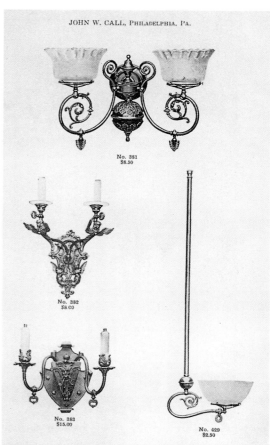

JOHN W. CALL, PHILADELPHIA, PA.

No. 381
$8.50

No. 382
$8.00

No. 383
$15.00

No. 429
$2.50

Gas brass wall brackets and pendant, circa 1900, from the John W. Call, Philadelphia, Gas Fixtures Catalogue. No. 381: $375-$550; No. 382: $325-$525; No. 383: $250-$475; No. 429: $250-$400.

Two lamps with original frosted shades decorated with amber overlay made approximately one decade apart. Left: Circa 1850, 5" diameter slate base, 12" tall to the burner, stem has its original gold tone finish. Original fishtail burner is marked A.H. Wood and was patented on November 9, 1852. $400-$500. Right: Circa 1860, 6" diameter base, this spelter and brass lamp with its original verde finish has the Greek key design, a popular classic motif. It has an Argand gas burner patented by J.E. Stanwood on August 3, 1858. $450-$550.

Circa 1880, porcelain and acid treated brass in the style of the Aesthetic movement, 15" tall to its original Argand burner. This lamp's period white opal glass ball shade with 2 1/4" fitter rests in a Grecian shade holder. $325-$625.

Opposite page:
Two figural gas lamps circa 1870.
Left: Figural lamp of white metal with patinated finish, 18" tall on a 5 1/2" diameter square brown slate base. Manufactured by Mitchell, Vance & Co., it is No. 0112 in the 1876 catalogue. The section adjacent to the base as well as the removable sword are brass. It has an iron fishtail burner, common to early gas lighting. $425-$825.
Right: Made of white metal (stripped of its original finish), No. 0882 in the Mitchell, Vance Catalogue published in 1876 is 20" tall to burner on a 5" diameter slate base. Marked E.P. Gleason and patented December 17, 1867, the Argand gas burner with its original Argand chimney is a different size from an incandescent mantle chimney. Note the lever adjustment protruding from the base of the burner which was used to precisely control gas flow. The period double ring cone shade is 10" in diameter and matches the lamp with its acid etched scene of Romans. $550-$950.

40

The lamp at left taken apart. At the far left are the chimney, post gallery burner, and Bunsen tube. In front of the burner are the shade clips which hold the top shade in place. Easily separated from the lamp, these clips are often mistakenly discarded. The eye shade on this particular lamp was located after the lamp was initially purchased.

Classic Victorian ornate cast iron, 6" diameter base with steel pillar stem 11" tall, circa 1890. The 5" diameter cased green glass eye shade, which inversely mirrors the shape of the 10" diameter cased green glass shade resting above the Welsbach post gallery burner, was designed to protect the eye from the glare of the mantle. $450-$750.

Opposite page:
Circa 1890, oxidized brass and black painted steel; the shade clearly matches the base of this unique lamp with a 5" diameter base. It has an Argand burner with Grecian shade holder. The lamp shows some wear to the finish as a result of use and age. The hand painted 10" diameter shade was decorated using the combination of a transfer design applied to the opal glass which was then filled in with polychrome decoration by hand. $450-$700.

Next page, 42:
The brass shaft of this circa 1890 lamp was painted with layers of burgundy-tinted lacquer which were then accented with black along the reeded column. Measuring 9" to the base of the burner with a bottom diameter of 6", this lamp has one of the first Welsbach gallery burners, which is marked "Welsbach System Patented March 15th 1887." The chimney, which fits into the gallery, is marked "Gold, Made in Bohemia" and the period shade is decorated with gold and green hand painted water lilies with gilt accents. $400-$625.

Two figural lamps from the 1890s in different styles with two types of hoses for conveying the gas from the wall or ceiling to the lamp. Left: The Egyptian revival brass plated lamp, 14" tall to the burner, is resting on a footed raised base 6" in diameter. Its acid etched starburst cut period shade has a fitter size of 2 5/8" and the burner is a "Young American" type. It has an original spiral brass gas hose with rubber interior. Note: when incomplete, this particular style of lamp is often mistaken for a cigar lighter from the same era. $350-$700.

Right: Featuring Cupid and made of iron with bronze and brass plating along with oxidized highlights, this lamp is fitted with a post gallery burner (an old one brand new from the box) and a chimney marked "Welsbach." The top shade and matching eye shade are made of white satin glass decorated with pink, green, blue, and gray. With mint original finish, this portable appears essentially the same as it did in the stores 100 years ago. The replacement hose on the lamp is a substitute for the cloth covered hoses used during the era (it's actually an airbrush hose available from an Art Supply store). $800-$1050.

Circa 1900, still sporting its original mica canopy, this lamp is 11" tall and sits on an onyx base 5" in diameter. The "trademark Austria" chimney rests in a Welsbach post gallery burner. The top shade and closely matching eye shade have acid etched decoration. $375-$575.

Circa 1900, Art Nouveau figural white metal lamp with bronze finish, 19 1/2" tall to burner (there is damage to the woman's arm). The rectangular base dimensions are 5 1/2" x 6 1/2". Welsbach burner #63B with the large size 2 3/8" gallery fitter for unusual period ruby glass shade with gold foil overlay and crackle glass ruffled edge. $600-$900.

46

t

that ever shone on this earth.

Acetylene Light is so clear and pure, so free from color-fog that you can see pale blue or pale pink by it at night as clearly as you could in daylight.

It is so diffusive (far-carrying, wide-spreading) that you can read a newspaper 18 feet *away* from it when you could not read that same size of type 14 feet away from a Kerosene Lamp or Electric Light of the same identical candle-power.

Acetylene is so brilliant, so free from color-fog and soot, that only *one-tenth* as much flame is needed to give the same amount of light as would be needed of Kerosene light, Gasolene light, or City Gas light.

This means that Acetylene light produces only a fraction of the *heat* given off by Kerosene or Gasolene Lamps,—that it consumes only a fraction of the Oxygen in the air, and produces only a fraction of the poisonous Carbonic Acid Gas given off by Lamps in lighting.

September 19, 1907 article from *The Youth's Companion* entitled "Why Country Homes Need Better Light."

Opposite page:
Art Nouveau brass plated iron base with sunflower decoration, circa 1910, 8" in diameter. The gallery burner has a "Superior Best flint glass" chimney. The 12" diameter white satin glass shade is hand painted with gold and the colors of yellow, gray, and brown. This lamp is 24" in height. $675-$800.

CITY CONVENIENCES FOR THE COUNTRY DWELLER

The use of Blau-Gas will increase the *value* of any house which has not at present a satisfactory lighting and cooking system. More city residents will now wish to reside in the country, as they can procure the same convenience of light and heat to which they are accustomed in town, and Blau-Gas also solves the problem of keeping servants contented while in the country for the summer. For all-the-year-round residents in the country, particularly the farmer, it will bring to the long winter evenings a cheerfulness which will prove a widespread blessing.

From the Blaugas sales catalogue circa 1910.

Gasoline Lamps

The gasoline lamp had a metal tank at the base of the lamp, which contained gasoline. Air pressure forced the fuel up to the burner, where it was vaporized by the heat and mixed with air to form a gas. One could argue that gasoline lamps belong in the first section of this book, along with lamps that have fonts. However, when the fuel is actually burned, it is in a gaseous form. Gaso-line lamps were used primarily in rural areas during the early twentieth century up through the 1940s.

W.C. Coleman invented the "safe gasoline table lamp," with its own match-generating burner, in approximately 1900. Other gasoline lamp manufacturers include the Bostwick-Braun Company, which sold the "Quick-lite," and the Knight Light and Soda Fountain Company, which sold the "Sunray."

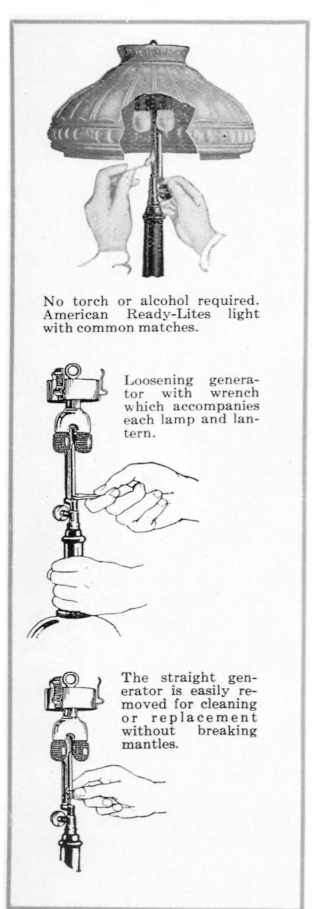

No torch or alcohol required. American Ready-Lites light with common matches.

Loosening generator with wrench which accompanies each lamp and lantern.

The straight generator is easily removed for cleaning or replacement without breaking mantles.

Style No. 321-M

With Ribbed Dome Opal Shade

WHO wou
nothing?
get your
This is how you
much oil as the
light. In other
lamps, you woul
the Sunray is ar
buy
vol
ter
only
The
the

The Sunray lamp made by the Knight Light & Soda Fountain Company circa 1900. $50-$175.

Ready-Lite Lamp made by the American Gas Machine Company, Inc. $50-$175.

49

Gas Fixture Styles

Gas fixtures were manufactured for over one hundred years. Although the design of oil lamps is limited by the necessity of having a fuel reservoir or font, gas fixture styles had no such limitation. Their design is primarily related to the time period in which they were manufactured and the type of home and room in which they were being used. There are both simple lightweight gas fixtures and heavy massive ornate gas fixtures.

There were, however, three technological improvements which altered the appearance of gas lighting: the large fitter shade, the incandescent mantle, and the inverted gas mantle burner.

In the mid-1870s it was recognized that openings at the bottom of larger shades provided more space for air to circulate around the gas burner and thus provided steadier light. Therefore, shades with a 2 5/8" fitting size, which were often hand blown and deeply etched, rapidly fell out of favor and fixtures were designed which used either 4" or 5" fitters. The 4" fitters eventually became more dominant.

The Welsbach mantle was introduced to the United States in 1890. Consisting of a cotton frame impreg

Selection of gas burners, mantles, and chimneys all in their original packing boxes. *Courtesy of The Gaslight Collection of Dan and Nancy Mattausch.*

nated with Thorium and Cerium, the mantle gave off an incandescent glow when heated. This put out much more light and allowed gas to compete with electric lighting for several more decades. The new mantles were used with gallery burners, which held the mantle over a Bunsen burner and had a built in chimney or shade holder. Gallery shades had no lip on the fitter, and came in two sizes: the common 1 7/8" and the rarer 2 3/8". Gallery burners were used with chimneys, as well as with dome, cone, and wave shades. A later development was the airhole chimney and the "Q" globes, which had holes on the side for more direct airflow to the mantle.

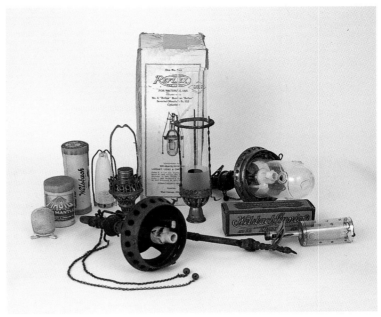

Selection of inverted and upright mantles and their boxes, including a Welsbach Jr. burner (mantle with built-in mica chimney) and a Welsbach No. 6 Reflex. *Courtesy of The Gaslight collection of Dan and Nancy Mattausch.*

COMBINATION NO. 4
Packed complete, one in a box, with Opal globe and shade and "GaSaver" mantle.

COMBINATION NO. 5
Packed complete, one in a box, with fancy hand-etched globe and "GaSaver" mantle.

COMBINATION NO. 6
Packed complete, one in a box, with "Q" globe and mantle.

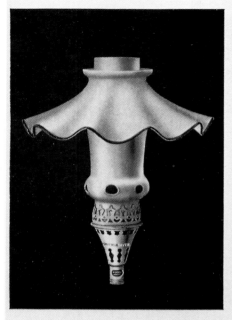

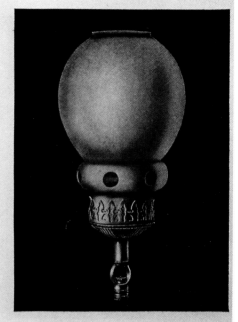

These shades are decorated on edge with either red, green or blue.
Price complete, as above, $18.00 per dozen.

Any of the fancy globes shown on page 16 may be substituted for one above shown, at same price.
Price complete, as above, $15.00 per dozen.

Price complete, as above, $7.20 per dozen.

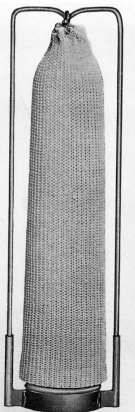

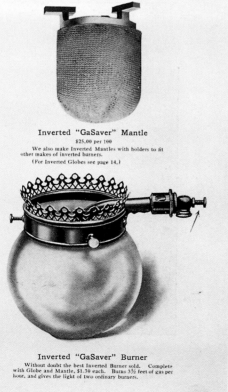

Inverted "GaSaver" Mantle
$25.00 per 100
We also make Inverted Mantles with holders to fit other makes of inverted burners.
(For Inverted Globes see page 14.)

Inverted "GaSaver" Burner
Without doubt the best Inverted Burner sold. Complete with Globe and Mantle, $1.30 each. Burns 3½ feet of gas per hour, and gives the light of two ordinary burners.

No. 44 6-in. Double Weave
For No. 6 Air Light Burner, $40 per 100
Retails at 35c.

"Gasaver" Mantles and Supplies from the F.A. Smith Manufacturing Co., Rochester, New York, circa 1900. Upright mantles, burners, and shades sold as one unit. $35-$85 each.

Additional "Gasaver" Mantles and Supplies from the F.A. Smith Manufacturing Co. Close-up of upright mantle, inverted mantle, and inverted gas burner. $5-$30 each.

The earliest gas burners include the rat-tail, cockspur, and cockscomb burners. By 1850 these were almost entirely replaced by the batswing, fishtail, and Argand gas burners. The batswing burner employed a small slit in a dome shaped top to spread the flame over a larger area. The fishtail burner used two single jets that impinged on each other, resulting in a more efficient flame. The circular Argand burner worked on the principle of allowing air to flow both within the center of the flame and outside the burner, as described in the previous chapter.

After many decades of experimentation, the inverted mantle was introduced in England in 1897. It became available in the United States in 1905. The inverted mantle used a breakthrough known as a thermostat to prevent gas, which wants to burn upward, from backfiring. Now gas fixtures could be made which cast their light downward, reducing shadows and providing more focused illumination. Inverted burners used a glass cylinder with holes inside the shade to direct air flow, similar to the purpose of chimneys on the upright burners. While these burners could be adapted to earlier fixtures with a "U" shaped goose neck, gas fixtures post 1897 were often designed with shades facing downwards and the shade sizes for these fixtures widened to the 3 1/4" size fitter.

In conclusion, ornate cast fixtures with hand-crafted details designed for use with smaller base shades are

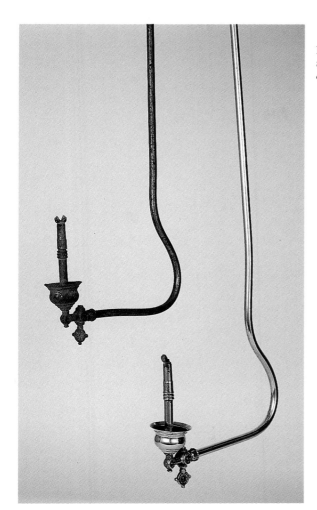

Pair of gas pendants circa 1890, one "in the rough" and one polished, 9" x 24". $65-$110 each. *Courtesy of Nadja Maril Historic Lighting.*

generally pre-1875. But there are overlaps in the usage of different styles. To a certain degree, fixture styles correspond to the style of furniture and decorative accessories of various eras in American nineteenth century design.

Opposite page:
Six arm electrified gas chandelier, circa 1880, bronze plating over base metal with decorative pieces of polished brass and original period frosted 4" shades. Diameter, 34"; hanging height, approximately 52". $2800-$4000. *Courtesy of Nadja Maril Historic Lighting.*

Three arm polished electrified gas fixture, circa 1890. Note the predominance of copper tones in this fixture due to the loss of zinc in the alloy combination; this is a result of age and repeated polishing. 34" diameter, 38" height from ceiling. $800-$1000. *Courtesy of Nadja Maril Historic Lighting.*

JOHN W. CALL, PHILADELPHIA, PA.

No. 362
$2.00

No. 375
With Candle, $4.50

No. 376
$4.50

No. 378
$2.25

No. 377
$1.25

Gas brackets from the John W. Call Gas Fixtures Catalogue "C", Philadelphia, Pennsylvania, circa 1890. No. 362: $185-$275; No. 375: $165-$225; No. 376: $285-$425; No. 378: $200-$300; No. 377 $130-$220.

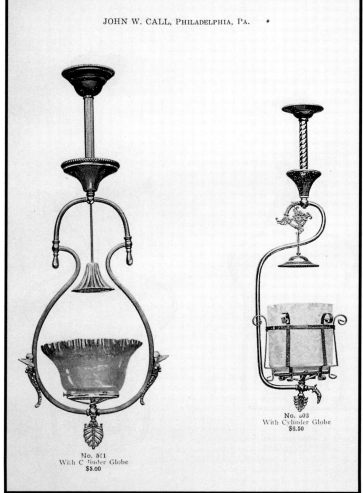

JOHN W. CALL, PHILADELPHIA, PA.

No. 541
With Cylinder Globe
$5.00

No. 503
With Cylinder Globe
$6.50

Hall lights from the John W. Call Gas Fixtures Catalogue "C", Philadelphia, Pennsylvania, circa 1890. No. 541: $450-$650; No. 503: $400-$600.

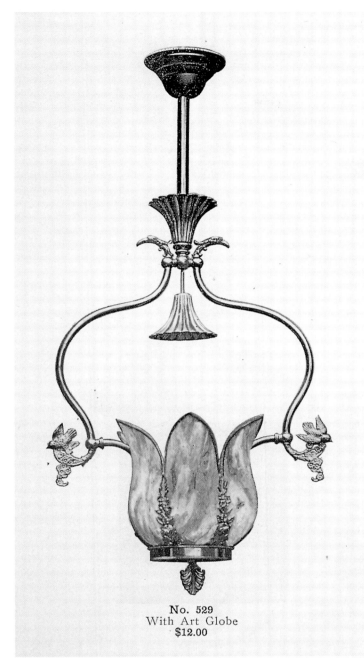

No. 529
With Art Globe
$12.00

Another hall light from the John W. Call Gas Fixtures Catalogue "C", Philadelphia, Pennsylvania, circa 1890. No. 529: $585-$800.

No. 620
1-light, $7.50

No. 631
1-light, $14.50

No. 630
1-light, $10.00

Newels from the John W. Call Gas Fixtures Catalogue "C", Philadelphia, Pennsylvania, circa 1890. These tall gas lamps would be affixed to the newel post of a front hall stairway. No. 620: $650-$800: No. 631: $650-$800; No. 630: $775-$1000.

Newels from the John W. Call Gas Fixtures Catalogue "C", Philadelphia, Pennsylvania, circa 1890. These figural gas lamps would also be affixed to the newel post of a front hall stairway. No. 619: $850-$1500; No. 618: $850-$1500.

No. 619
1-light, $38.00

No. 618
1-light, $25.00

No. 1032
2-light, $7.75
3-light, $10.00
4-light, $12.25

Three armed gas fixture with acid etched lacy shades from the John W. Call Gas Fixtures Catalogue "C", Philadelphia, Pennsylvania, circa 1890. $800-$1200.

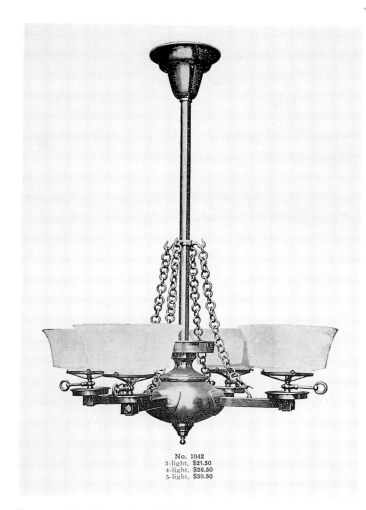

No. 1042
3-light, $23.50
4-light, $26.50
5-light, $30.50

Four armed gas fixture from the John W. Call Gas Fixtures Catalogue "C", Philadelphia, Pennsylvania, circa 1890. This fixture has square frosted shades, a precursor of the Arts and Crafts Style. $950-$1400.

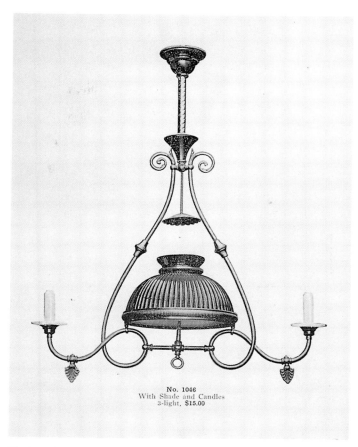

No. 1046
With Shade and Candles
3-light, $15.00

Shade and candle gas fixture from the John W. Call Gas Fixtures Catalogue "C", Philadelphia, Pennsylvania, circa 1890. $800-$1200.

No. 1052
3-light, $19.00
Complete

Art glass shade and candle gas fixture from the John W. Call Gas Fixtures Catalogue "C", Philadelphia, Pennsylvania, circa 1890. $750-$1200.

Left and below: Nickel plated brass gas light oculist bracket, patented May 21, 1889, with turn of the century Welsbach gallery; missing its air deflector. This class of brackets enabled the optician, dentist, or doctor to move the light vertically as well as horizontally in order to closely focus light on his work. 43" x 12". $350-600. *Collection of Erich Haesche.*

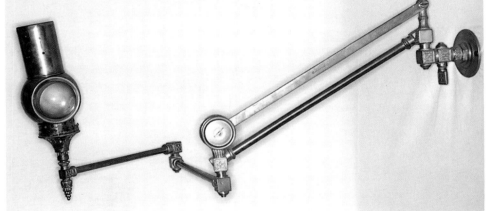

Gas portable lamp, circa 1910. With a shade of curved green slag glass panels (termed art glass during the era), this lamp is made of spiral brass tubing and black marble and has a period mica chimney. The valve attached to this lamp is the safety valve from a portable gas heater, an example of how lamps are often inaccurately modified. $275-$600. *Collection of Eric Haesche.*

Inverted, two arm gas fixture, "in the rough", circa 1900. The orange and green flowers painted onto the molded frosted period shades were fired onto the inside of the glass. 22" x 26". $200-450. *Courtesy of Nadja Maril Historic Lighting.*

Circa 1910, nickel plated lamp by the Badger Brass Company with the model name of "Solar," 6 1/2" x 12". This unique lamp was designed to make its own acetylene gas by mixing carbide and water. The carbide was placed inside a central cylinder while the water was placed in the bottom of the lamp's interior. The cylinder was lowered into the water to keep the mixture going. No chimney is needed with this lamp, which uses an acetylene gas burner. While not original to the lamp, the period 10" banquet lamp globe with 4" fitter is made of frosted glass with an applied overlay of pink glass in the motif of irises. $275-$450. *Courtesy of The Gaslight Collection of Dan and Nancy Mattausch.*

Below: Two arm electrified gas fixture with original gilded finish over brass, circa 1920. Period hand blown inverted thumb print opalescent glass shades, 26" x 30". $600-$850. *Courtesy of Nadja Maril Historic Lighting.*

Chapter Four
Lamps Which Use Electricity

Electricity 1879 to the Present

Many antique collectors have the mistaken impression that if a lamp has always been used with electricity it must not be very old and certainly has very little value. These are the folks who would rather purchase a new crystal chandelier or a new lamp made from a supposedly antique jar or vase rather than an authentic fixture from the early twentieth century.

By definition, early electric lamps and fixtures are antiques because they are over one hundred years old. The first successful incandescent light bulb was invented in 1879. The first power station was located at Holborn Viaduct in London in 1880, and in 1882 the Pearl Street Station in New York began providing electricity to customers, including the *New York Times* editorial and lighting rooms. During the 1890s many companies which had previously manufactured lighting powered by kerosene and gas now included electric lamps and fixtures in their line of products.

The earliest electric fixtures look a lot like gas fixtures minus the gas valves. Poles, not chains, are used. Tubular arms join electric sockets to the main body of lamps, wall brackets, and hanging fixtures referred to as electroliers. Many lamps and fixtures featured bare bulbs, because they were considered an exciting new invention worthy of direct admiration. When shades were used, they did not necessarily cover the bulb and they were held in place by a fitting that was attached to the electric sockets and designed to hold the 2 1/4" shade in place. The unicap fitters used three tiny screws while others used wire clips.

During this early era of electric use many fixtures were made which relied on a combination of gas and electric power. Electricity was considered potentially unreliable, so the combination of gas and electricity was both modern and practical. Combination gas and electric fixtures can be identified by the combination of arms designed for electricity and gas. The early classic fixtures of this type have the gas arms facing up and the electric arms facing down. Those using inverted gas have both the electric and gas lights focused downwards.

Because combination fixtures are very desirable, additional arms are often added to the body of a fixture in disrepair to create a pseudo gas and electric combination.

Sometimes electric arms are turned upwards and fitted with 4" shade holders and gas shades. Look to see if the style and proportion of the arms are appropriate to the dimensions of the fixture's body.

As with gas and kerosene fixtures, technological advances required patents. Competition between companies was fierce as they competed for a share of the marketplace. Places to look for patents with the date and company's name include electric sockets, shade holders and shades, the canopy, and any special adjustment mechanisms.

The early light bulbs were made of clear glass. Bulbs made before 1920 had a small tip on the end, a result of sealing the bulb after the air was pumped out. After 1920, a glass exhaust tube incorporated into the center stem created the rounded shape with which we are familiar today. Frosted bulbs were not made until approximately 1925.

The first light bulbs cast a dim light, which reduced any need for a shade or covering on the bulb. Lamps with a variety of adjustments, enabling one to focus light where it was needed, were popular at the beginning of electricity's use.

A larger market for electric fixtures was created with the introduction of the tungsten filament in 1907 and the Mazda lamp, first marketed in 1910.

Electricity gave designers further opportunities for artistic expression. The early twentieth century is the era of beautiful reverse painted shades and leaded glass lamps. Multiple sockets for two or three light bulbs provided the ability to uniformly illuminate unusual hand-crafted shades. These types of lamps had been made for kerosene and gas, but with the advent of electricity they flourished.

Unusual shapes and sizes were possible; these included flat mounted wall lights with glass covers, as well as figural lamps with round shades which sat on top of radios during the 1920s and 30s. Different shaped bulbs introduced during the mid-1930s included bulbs resembling the bud shape (we now call them chandelier bulbs); there was also a resurgence of fixtures and lamps which featured exposed bulbs. Sometimes light

The G. E. Tungsten Lamp

gives the most pleasing artificial light obtainable and uses LESS THAN HALF the current of former incandescent lamps

3843

bulbs were covered with a net of beads, at other times they had small silk shades.

While the era of electricity provided the freedom to build lamps in new configurations and styles, this same era also saw a number of strong revivals attempting to re-create looks from the past. There were lamps made to look like candle fixtures in addition to whale oil and Argand lamps. Entire style lines were developed to mimic different looks, from lanterns hanging in Gothic castles to solar lamp fixtures with graceful crystals.

Advertising card for the G.E. Tungsten Lamp, circa 1907.

Three armed early electric polished and rewired chandelier, circa 1895, with period acid etched shades. Unicap fitters, original Bakelite turn switches, and straight pole and filigree castings identify this fixture as being made at the beginning of the electric era. 34" x 29". $675-$900. *Courtesy of Nadja Maril Historic Lighting.*

Pair of two arm early electric polished rewired fixtures, circa 1895, 21" x 44". Shown with two different pairs of period shades: one set is cut and frosted by an unidentified company; the other set is frosted and clear pattern glass by the Gillinder Company. $365-475 each. *Courtesy of Nadja Maril Historic Lighting.*

Opposite page:
Early electric hall lamp, brass with original patina and long cut crystals (some damaged), circa 1900, similar in design and feeling to kerosene and gas lamps of the same era. 10" x 40". $750-900. *Courtesy of Nadja Maril Historic Lighting.*

Gas and electric hall lamp, circa 1900. Polished brass, rewired with period opal glass candle and drip cup as well as period opal glass shade, 12" x 30". $375-$575. *Courtesy of Nadja Maril Historic Lighting.*

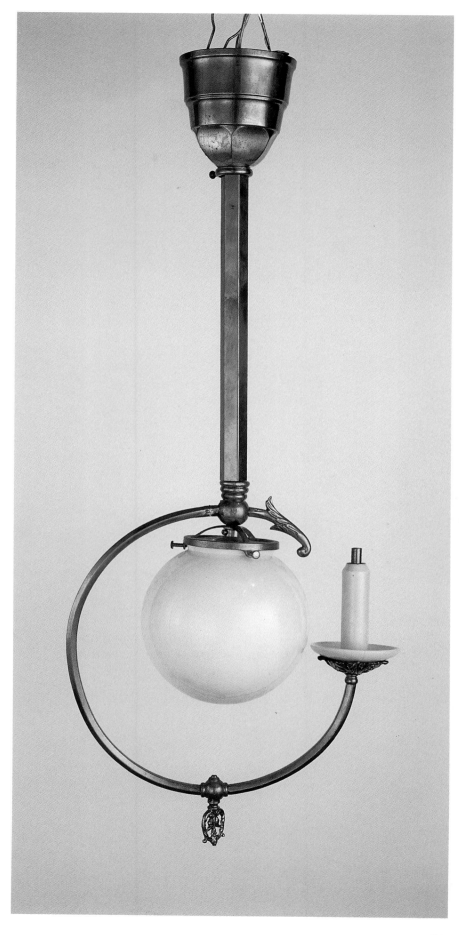

Opposite page:
Combination four arm brass gas and electric fixture, electrified with altered bell socket shade holders (the originals would have been an open fitter with the socket visible). Period pattern glass panel and starburst shades. Circa 1900, 20" x 29". $800-$1000. *Courtesy of Nadja Maril Historic Lighting.*

SOCKETS
KEYLESS

Same as No. 4 except without key.

Yost

Each
No. 40BB—Brush brass finish, ⅛ in....$0.50
No. 40OC—Ox. copper finish, ⅛ in...... .55
No. 40N—Nickel finish, ⅛ in.......... .55
Twenty-Five in a Box

PENDANT

A great advantage is the composition bushing in cap which gives a large opening, 13-32 inch diameter, ample to admit duplex or reinforced cord, avoiding expense of using ⅜-inch cap and inserting the usual threaded composition bushing. This saves expense of extra bushing and labor of installing.

Yost

No. 400BB—Brush brass finish....Each $0.50
Twenty-Five in a Box

CHAIN PULL

A high-grade socket of the new and convenient chain pull construction. Chain about 8 inches long.

Yost

Each
No. 45BB—Brush brass finish, ⅛ in.....$0.60
No. 45OC—Ox. copper finish, ⅛ in...... .65
No. 45N—Nickel finish, ⅛ in......... .65
Twenty-Five in a Box

An electric socket with Bryant Bakelite turn switch with the patent date of June 13, 1899. The attached spring mechanism shade holder was patented February 23, 1904. These markings are difficult to see when the brass has darkened with age, but are very important in helping to authenticate a lamp.

 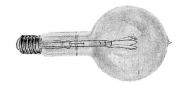

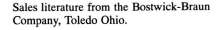

Sales literature from the Bostwick-Braun Company, Toledo Ohio.

Sales literature from the Bostwick-Braun Company, Toledo, Ohio.

Green and caramel glass desk lamp with original patina, dated October 20, 1909, rewired with replaced socket and switch. 9" x 15". $475-$600. *Collection of Nadja Maril.*

Handel table lamp, circa 1914, rewired but otherwise all original. The 18" brown shade has an acid cutback design of bamboo and is numbered and patented on the interior, No. 6200 and US patent 77618. It has the signed Handel interlocking shade ring at the top. The foot of this oriental style base with original matte bronze finish resembles a Chinese carved and pierced hardwood stand. 7" x 26". $3800-$5200. *Courtesy of Nadja Maril Historic Lighting.*

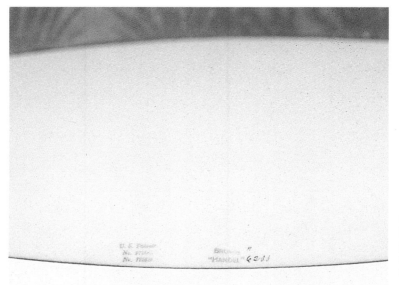

Close-up of the interior Handel shade shown in the previous photograph, revealing the numbered signature and patent number.

From the Gimbel Brothers 1922-23 season catalogue.

Opposite page:
Advertisement for Handel Lamps, circa 1920. The Handel Company, located in Meriden, Connecticut, first opened for business in 1885 and started selling electric lamps and fixtures in 1892. They remained in business until 1936.

Jefferson table lamp, circa 1920. The 16" reverse painted scenic globe is signed and numbered 2907. The rewired base has original patina and double pull chain sockets. 23" x 6". $1800-$2200.
Collection of Christopher J. Patrick.

Polished brass double socket lamp with pull chain, patented 1911, 7" x 20". Original period cased green glass mushroom globe, 10" diameter. $775-$995. *Courtesy of Nadja Maril Historic Lighting.*

Bronze plated lamp with square Art Nouveau design base, circa 1915, 7" x 20". Period amber crackle glass mushroom globe, 10" diameter. $600-$860. *Courtesy of Nadja Maril Historic Lighting.*

Moe Bridges, reverse painted, signed scenic table lamp, circa 1915. Signed on the 14" shade and base, this double socketed lamp has been rewired but is otherwise in original condition. 22" x 6". $2000-$2800. *Courtesy of Nadja Maril Historic Lighting.*

Edward Miller & Company brass and cast metal table lamp with decorated glass shade. Although the 18" shade is not signed, it is easy to see that it is original to this lamp as the ribbed design of the shade corresponds to the design of the base. Blown into a mold, the shade's interior is a glossy white opal; the exterior has a fired on orange matte finish. The rewired base is signed "E.M. Co.", and the sockets have been replaced. $900-$1650. *Courtesy of Nadja Maril Historic Lighting..*

1925 advertisement for the Miller Lamp Company.

Selections from The Milhender Book of Lamps and Appliances, Catalogue 3, Boston Massachusetts, circa 1918. No. L822: $800-$1100; No. L2115: $265-$350; No. L2408: $265-$350.

Opposite page:
Transfer painted scenic table lamp, circa 1920, with original patina and single pull chain socket. 16" diameter shade, base 22" x 7 1/2". $1400-$1800. *Collection of Justin M. Patrick.*

Silhouette lamp, circa 1915, with bent caramel slag glass panels and illuminated base, rewired with triple sockets. 18" x 20" x 8 1/2". $700-$1200. *Courtesy of The Stock Exchange, Easton, Maryland.*

No. L 1499½

From the Milhender Book of Lamps and Appliances, Catalogue C, Boston, Massachusetts, circa 1918. $2400-$3500.

Selections from The Milhender Book of Lamps and Appliances, Catalogue 3, Boston Massachusetts, circa 1918. No. L746: $750-$950; No. L796: $575-$850; No. L743: $600-$850.

No. L 3379
Height: 17 inches.
Price $26.00.

No. L 3339
Height: 27 inches.
Price $39.00.

No. L 3389
Height: 17 inches.
Price $30.00.

Bronze figural electric lamps from the Milhender Book of Lamps and Appliances, Catalogue C, Boston, Massachusetts, circa 1918. No. L3389: $550-$900; No. L3339: $650-$1000.

Art Nouveau five arm brass chandelier, circa 1910, with signed Quezel art glass shades, 26" x 62". The Quezel Art Glass and Decorating Company was founded in 1901 in Brooklyn, New York by former Tiffany decorator Martin Bach and closed in 1924. This unusual fixture has the fluid elements of the French Art Nouveau movement, which influenced design in America from approximately 1890-1920. $2800-$4000. *Courtesy of Nadja Maril Historic Lighting.*

Consolidated Glass Company reverse painted molded grape chandelier marked with patent #40893 and dated September 20, 1910. The rewired fixture has a gold brass finish, original lacquer coating, deteriorated original chain, and original P & S Bakelite turn switches. 17" x 29". $2600-$3800. *Courtesy of Nadja Maril Historic Lighting.*

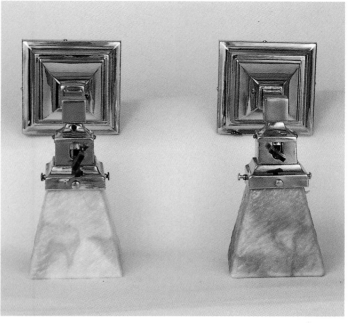

18" inverted satin glass dome with taupe, rust, and green stencil applied decoration and glossy white interior, circa 1915. This fixture is "in the rough" and currently has no electric components. $140-$300. *Courtesy of Nadja Maril Historic Lighting.*

Mission style electric wall brackets. Rewired, polished, and lacquered with original levithon switches, circa 1915; frosted period shades. $300-$450 for the pair. *Courtesy of Taylor Wells Antiques, Riverdale Maryland.*

Mission style two arm chandelier, circa 1915. Polished brass, lacquered and rewired with original turn switches marked levithon, 20" x 15"; original period frosted shades. This is a popular style which is associated with the Arts and Crafts Movement popularized in America by American furniture maker Gustav Stickley; it is sometimes hard to distinguish the reproductions of these square fixtures from the originals. Look for original electric hardware as well as narrow bands of brass inside the ceiling mount used as a reinforcement in the originals. $385-$600. *Courtesy of Taylor Wells Antiques, Riverdale, Maryland.*

Five arm Mission style polished and rewired electric chandelier, circa 1920, with period square frosted shades and original Bakelite turn switches marked Bryant. 22" x 32". $550-$750. *Courtesy of Nadja Maril Historic Lighting.*

Pairpoint Decorative Arts Lamp, circa 1920. Located in New Bedford, Massachusetts, the company was incorporated in 1894 and closed in 1938. Featuring a multi-colored background of green waves, the 16" diameter reverse painted glass shade was hand painted with lavender, mauve, red, and gold flowers fired on to the glass, The black marble and brass base with original wiring and three candle sockets is 28" x 6". $5000-$6500. *Courtesy of Nadja Maril Historic Lighting.*

Regency revival style 1930s rewired table lamp. Reverse painted glass panels sit inside a white metal frame, 18" in diameter. There was a center interior shade, probably of white opal glass, which is missing; there is also some damage to the base. The panels were reverse painted using a stencil. This was a less expensive version of the Pairpoint Fine Arts Lamp shown in the previous photograph, made by a competing manufacturer. $500-$875. *Courtesy of Nadja Maril Historic Lighting.*

Pair of two light candlestick lamps with original wiring, circa 1922. Designed for use on a mantelpiece or sideboard, these lamps measure 26" x 14". $275-$450 for the pair. *Courtesy of Nadja Maril Historic Lighting.*

From the Gimbel Brothers Catalogue for the 1922-23 season.

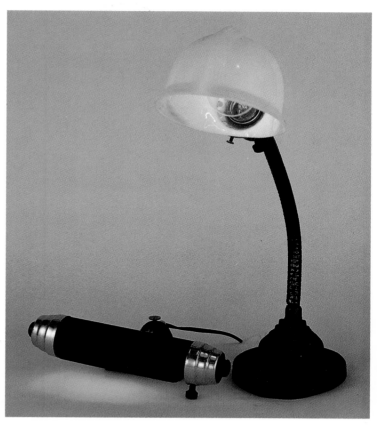

Left: A textured finish was coated onto this metal tubular reading lamp with chrome accents. 4" x 12", it has its original wiring and socket circa 1940. $25-$75. Right: Goose neck metal desk lamp with textured bronze finish and period opal glass shade, circa 1935. 14" x 6". $35-$85. *Courtesy of Nadja Maril Historic Lighting.*

Desk and reading lamps from the Milhender Book of Lamps and Appliances, Catalogue C, Boston, Massachusetts, circa 1918. No. L1459: $265-$375; No. L1584: $650-$950; No. L1469: $225-$325; No. L95: $75-$150; No. L75: $110-$200; No. L85: $90-$160.

Emeralite 8734 desk lamps with rounded and square brass bases, patented 1916. Square based Emeralite has a satin finish; the socket has been replaced and the identification plate is missing, but it still has remnants of the original label on the back of the shade. 8" x 14". $475-$650. Round based Emeralite has the bright finish and all its original components. $525-$750. *Courtesy of Nadja Maril Historic Lighting.*

Double breadloaf cased green shaded lamp, designed for a partner's desk with original finish, rewired with replaced sockets. This lamp is probably a Greenalite (competitor of the Emeralite line). 8" x 18". $900-$1200. *Courtesy of Nadja Maril Historic Lighting.*

Eyes Need This Light

GLARING or misplaced lights hurt the eyes and hasten fatigue. They behave better and last longer when working in a light that suits them.

Emeralites keep minds alert by resting the eyes. Your business needs them to promote comfort and efficiency. Your home needs them for reading, writing or sewing.

Nature made green and daylight restful to eyes. That's why Emeralite has an Emerald Glass Shade and a special screen that changes ordinary electric light into soft, eye-saving daylite.

Most lighting fixtures designed for home use, are not suitable for reading or study. Emeralites look well, harmonize with any environment and provide the best working light.

Emeralite Bed Lamp
[Fits Any Bed]
Makes reading in bed delightful. The Emerald Glass Shade reflects a soft glow where you need it and eliminates glare. Has dimming socket with four changes of light—down to a mereglow for sick-room or night light.

Emeralite Junior
For those places the big lights don't reach. Adjustable green shade protects the eyes from glare. Just the light for reading, writing, sewing or study. Stands, hangs or clamps anywhere.

Emeralite Floor Lamp
Your eyes will enjoy this chair-side companion. Has telescoping stand, adjustable shade and daylitescreen. Ideal for bridge, reading, sewing, writing, etc.

There is an Emeralite for every place and purpose. Booklet showing complete line in colors sent free upon request.

Genuine Emeralites are branded for your protection, and have the Emerald Glass Shade with the Daylite Screen. Buy them by name from department stores, office supply and electrical dealers.

H. G. McFADDIN & CO., 34 Warren St., N. Y.
Established 1874

EMERALITE
KIND TO EYES

A pan style 1920s chandelier, rewired and polished, of higher quality then the pair on page 86. The chain and the arms are heavier and the body is made of three sections rather than two. Shown with period art glass shades, signed Quezel. $950-$1150. *Courtesy of Nadja Maril Historic Lighting.*

Advertisement for Emeralite lamps, circa 1924.

Two polished, rewired brass pan chandeliers, circa 1920. These are referred to as pan chandeliers because they were manufactured by using sheets of brass which were pressed into shape. Before being fitted together, the top and bottom mid-sections resemble the lid of a pan. The five arm 18" diameter fixture on the left, with original Levithon Bakelite turn switches, has period frosted shades which were molded to resembled fabric shades with tassels. $465-$585. The four arm 16" diameter fixture on the right has replaced sockets and switches as well as period hand painted scenic shades imported from Czechoslovakia, popular in the 1920s and 30s. $425-$565. *Courtesy of Nadja Maril Historic Lighting.*

Four polished and rewired brass pendant fixtures from the early twentieth century with period signed Holophane prismatic shades. The earliest fixture is the straight pole with the unicap fitter and long pull chain, dated 1905. The first homes with electricity did not have central wall switches so the pull chain was very important for reaching up and turning on the light. The chain pendants are from approximately 1915 to 1930. Values for fixture and shade, from left to right: $125-$180, $130-$175, $115-$170, $120-$175. *Courtesy of Nadja Maril Historic Lighting.*

Pan chandelier with large central dome and four lights. Cupids and rams' heads ornament this 24" diameter fixture; made of polished and lacquered brass as well as cast white metal which has been plated brass. The period frosted shades have cut starburst decoration. Rewired, the original Bakelite switches are marked "paiste." $575-$800. *Courtesy of Taylor Wells Antiques, Riverdale, Maryland.*

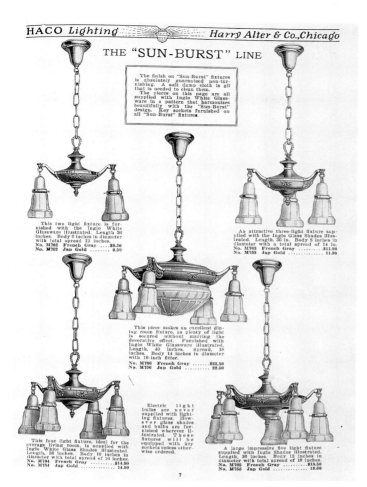

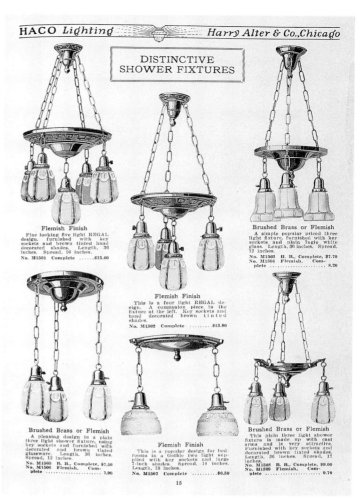

Solid brass fixtures with the exception of the chains, these "pan" fixtures were sold with a coated finish advertised as non tarnishing. From the 1924 Haco Lighting Fixtures Catalogue "M". $195-$575.

Another type of fixture inexpensively mass produced was the "Shower Fixture." From the 1924 Haco Lighting Fixtures Catalogue "M". $150-$450.

Polished, rewired brass shower fixture, circa 1920, with original period frosted shades and original Bakelite turn switches marked Arrow. 12" x 13 1/2". $175-$295. *Courtesy of Rebecca L. Rydbom.*

The Gothic Revival was popular during the 1920s, as demonstrated by the torchiere and chandelier in this 1926 *Country Life* advertisement for radiator covers.

Three electric wall brackets, circa 1905. The fixture on the far left is polished brass, rewired with period frosted geometric decorated shade and has the long pull chain indicative of an earlier electric fixture. $110-$165. The bottom fixture, in the rough, has a period Holophane clear glass shade and was a portable designed to be hooked onto the wall rather than permanently installed. $48-$85. The fixture on the far right, with acid etched period shade, has been polished and rewired and is marked "Edison Patents" on the socket. 6" x 12". $140-$195. *Courtesy of Nadja Maril Historic Lighting.*

Pair of heavy brass double light sconces, representing a transition from the Classic Victorian to the Colonial Revival style, circa 1920. Measuring 15" x 18", they are shown with period combination clear pattern glass and frosted glass shades. $400-$545 for the pair. *Courtesy of Nadja Maril Historic Lighting.*

A trio of two light sconces from the late 1920s to early 1930s, all rewired. The top left is polished brass. The bottom fixture is plated brass and is the original finish. The top right fixture has the original black enamel finish and original parchment shades. Each sconce measures approximately 14" x 16". $65-$125 each. *Courtesy of Nadja Maril Historic Lighting.*

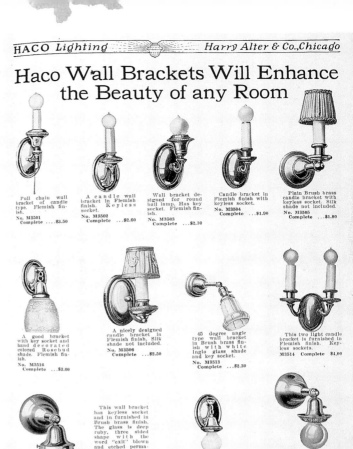

Haco Wall Brackets Will Enhance the Beauty of any Room

Pull chain wall bracket of candle type. Flemish finish.
No. M3501 Complete $3.50

A candle wall bracket in Flemish finish. Keyless socket.
No. M3502 Complete ...$2.60

Wall bracket designed for round ball lamp. Has key socket. Flemish finish.
No. M3503 Complete ...$2.10

Candle bracket in Flemish finish with keyless socket.
No. M3504 Complete ...$1.90

Plain Brush brass candle bracket with keyless socket. Silk shade not included.
No. M3505 Complete ...$1.80

A good bracket with key socket and hand decorated colored Rosebud shade. Flemish finish.
No. M3516 Complete ...$3.00

A nicely designed candle bracket in Flemish finish. Silk shade not included.
No. M3506 Complete ...$2.50

45 degree angle type wall bracket in Brush brass finish with white Inglo glass shade and key socket.
No. M3513 Complete ...$2.30

This two light candle bracket is furnished in Flemish finish. Keyless sockets.
M3514 Complete $4.00

This wall bracket has keyless socket and is furnished in Brush brass finish. The glass is deep ruby, three sided shape with the word "exit" blown and etched permanently in the glass. All building codes require an exit light of this type in theaters, halls, hotels and all public buildings.
No. M3517 Complete ...$5.50

A neat drop bracket in ball husk type. Key socket Flemish finish.
No. M3515 Complete $2.20

This ball husk type bracket has key socket and is furnished in all finishes.

No.	Finish	Complete
M3507	Brush Brass	$2.20
M3508	Flemish	2.30
M3509	Nickel	2.30
M3510	White Enamel	2.40
M3511	French Gray	2.40
M3512	Jap Gold	2.40

35

Above: Close-up of the back of the Bradley and Hubbard sconces below, showing the B & H signature.

Top right: Some of the many different wall brackets sold in 1924 as shown in the Haco Lighting Fixtures Catalog "M".

Below: Elegant, signed Bradley and Hubbard electric fixtures, circa 1925. Polished and rewired, the two sconces have pull chain mechanisms for the candle socket; these mechanisms are no longer in production. 16" x 18". $585-$700 for the pair. *Courtesy of Nadja Maril Historic Lighting.*

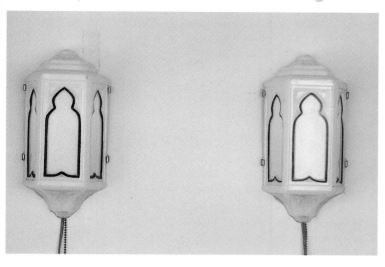

Art Deco style wall sconces, circa 1930. White glass with painted black decoration slides over a metal back plate. Rewired with new sockets. 7" x 12". $300-$425 pair. *Courtesy of Nadja Maril Historic Lighting.*

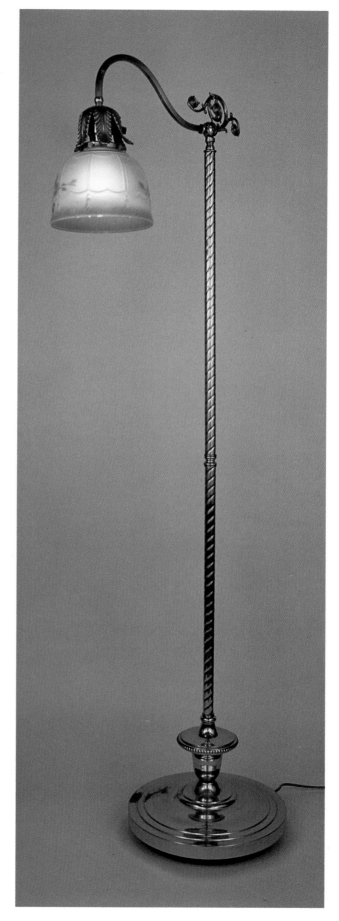

Polished and lacquered floor lamp, circa 1920, with adjustable arm; rewired with new socket. This style lamp was often used with a beaded and fringed silk shade, of which very few originals have survived. 15" x 54", it is shown with a period frosted and hand painted glass shade. $200-$325. *Collection of Nadja Maril.*

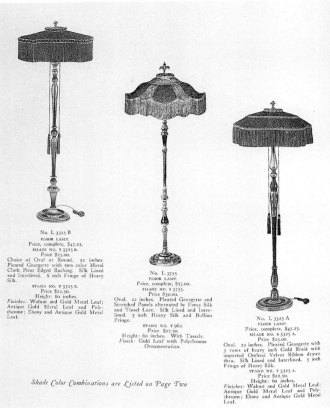

No. L 2012
BRIDGE LAMP.
Price, complete, $16.75.
SHADE NO. S 2012.
Price $15.00.
14 inches. Shirred Georgette with panels of Gold Trimmed Lace. Silk Lined. 6 inch Fringe of Heavy Silk.
STAND NO. T 8100.
Price $22.25.
Height: 55 inches. Fluted Stem.
Finish: Tones of Brown. Stippled Base.

No. L 6050
BRIDGE LAMP.
Price, complete, $34.50.
SHADE NO. S 6050.
Price $14.00.
14 inches. Shirred Georgette with panels of Embroidered Lace. Silk Lined. 6 inch Fringe of Heavy Silk.
STAND NO. T 7671.
Price $21.00.
Height: 55 inches.
Finish: Polychrome.

No. L 7100
BRIDGE LAMP.
Price, complete, $43.00.
SHADE NO. S 7000.
Price $15.50.
12 inch. Pleated Georgette Sides with Metal Brocade Top. Silk Lined.
STAND NO. T 910.
Price $27.75.
Height: 55 inches.
Finish: Gold Leaf and Polychrome.

No. L 3325 B
FLOOR LAMP.
Price, complete, $47.25.
SHADE NO. S 3325 B.
Price $25.00.
Choice of Oval or Round. 22 inches. Pleated Georgette with two color Metal Cloth Picot Edged Ruching. Silk Lined and Interlined. 6 inch Fringe of Heavy Silk.
STAND NO. T 3325 B.
Price $22.50.
Height: 60 inches.
Finishes: Walnut and Gold Metal Leaf; Antique Gold Metal Leaf and Polychrome; Ebony and Antique Gold Metal Leaf.

No. L 3755
FLOOR LAMP.
Price, complete, $57.00.
SHADE NO. S 3755.
Price $30.00.
Oval. 22 inches. Pleated Georgette and Stretched Panels alternated by Fancy Silk and Tinsel Lace. Silk Lined and Interlined. 5 inch Heavy Silk and Bullion Fringe.
STAND NO. T 962.
Price $27.50.
Height: 60 inches. With Tassels.
Finish: Gold Leaf with Polychrome Ornamentation.

No. L 3325 A
FLOOR LAMP.
Price, complete, $47.25.
SHADE NO. S 3325 A.
Price $25.00.
Oval. 22 inches. Pleated Georgette with 3 rows of heavy inch Gold Braid with imported Ombrai Velvet Ribbon drawn thru. Silk Lined and Interlined. 5 inch Fringe of Heavy Silk.
STAND NO. T 3325 A.
Price $22.50.
Height: 60 inches.
Finishes: Walnut and Gold Metal Leaf; Antique Gold Metal Leaf and Polychrome; Ebony and Antique Gold Metal Leaf.

Shade Color Combinations are Listed on Page Two

Milhender Electric Supply Company floor lamps. $275-$400 each.

Milhender Electric Supply Company floor lamps. $300-$425 each, complete.

A selection of electric ceiling mounts and decorative bulb holders, circa 1920. The four ceiling mounts in the back row of this photograph were designed to be used with bare bulbs and demonstrate a variety of textures and finishes, from stamped and shiny brass to a deep bronze tone. The bulb ornaments in the front of the picture were put on chandeliers to enhance the appearance of bare bulbs. They are often removed by dealers in order to attach glass shades to fixtures so they will be more appealing to customers. $5-$45 each. *Courtesy of Nadja Maril Historic Lighting.*

*L*ight your rooms
for comfort—and for beauty

Mere charm of appearance is not enough—good light is not enough. A lamp—a real lamp—must have both. Miller lamps are designed for symmetry, for charm of color and line—and for greatest lighting efficiency.

They form a glowing center for the activity of the room. They add their warm tones to its beauty—their true light to its comfort.

And it is always pleasant to meet the low prices made possible by the great Miller production. See these—and other—Miller lamps at your Lighting Company. Ask for them by name.

THE MILLER COMPANY, *Meriden, Conn.*

MILLER
LAMPS

L 120

L 2801

L 115

Crystal bead fixture, circa 1925, 14" diameter with replaced brass ceiling mount. To see how this fixture originally looked, study fixture No. 492 of the Crystal Line in the following illustration. $175-$295. *Courtesy of Nadja Maril Historic Lighting.*

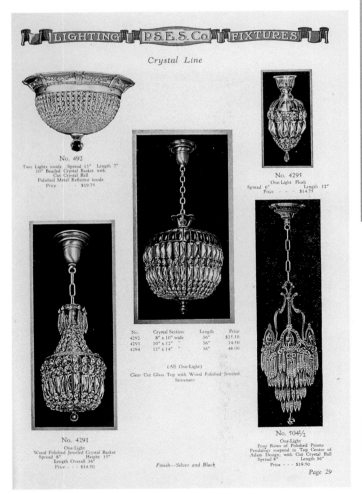

10" diameter molded clear glass shade with flying geese pattern, probably meant for a kitchen or bathroom, circa 1920. The re-silvered metal cylinder, originally chrome plated, contains the bulb. $48-$110. *Courtesy of Nadja Maril Historic Lighting.*

Public Service Electrical Supply Co. Inc. Catalogue, Baltimore, Maryland, circa 1925. No. 492: $225-$325; No. 4291: $250-$350; No. 4292-94: $250-$400; No. 4295: $75-$125; No. 504 1/2: $265-$375.

Two brass rewired pendant fixtures with original shades from the 1920s. Fixture on the left has been polished; the shade has an applied stencil decoration. $175-$285. Fixture on the right has original finish and the shade is colored molded glass. $195-$300. *Courtesy of Nadja Maril Historic Lighting.*

Holophane "Hat fixture," signed on the glass shade rim with original chrome fitting, circa 1935. These fixtures and similar ones were used in commercial institutions and businesses into the 1940s. The Holophane Lighting Corporation was bought out by the Manville Corporation in 1974. The contemporary versions of Holophane Shades, which do not include this particular design, are clear glass and not of the same quality associated with Holophane shades made at the beginning of the century. 12" x 18". $50-$175. *Courtesy of Nadja Maril Historic Lighting.*

Polished, rewired brass fixture, circa 1925, designed for commercial use. 64" x 21". $250-$550. *Courtesy of Ruby Lively Kelly.*

Art Deco fixture, circa 1925, pot metal with "antique silver" finish. Designed, as with the previous fixture, for use with exposed light bulbs, 52" x 22". $125-$265. *Courtesy of Ruby Lively Kelly.*

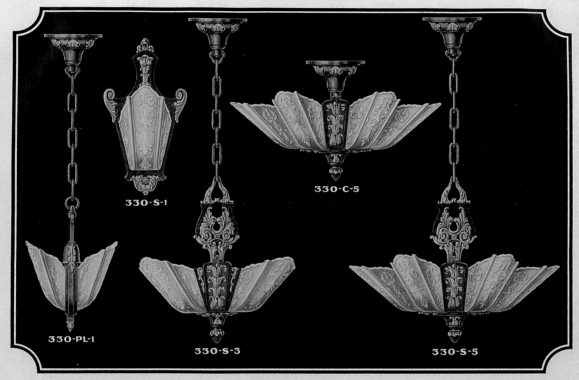

330-S-1

330-C-5

330-PL-1

330-S-3

330-S-5

Quiet dignity—delicate tracery of design artistically embellished in plated Etruscan Gold.

Etruscan Series

No. 330-PL-1. One light Pendant Lantern. Spread 6¾x8½ inches. Length 36 inches. *Price $6.90.*

NOTE: No. 330-PL-1 can be changed to a Ceiling Style, if desired, by eliminating the chain.

No. 330-S-1. One light Wall Bracket. Backplate 6½x12 inches. Covers 4-inch outlet. Extension 5 inches. Canopy switch control. *Price $4.50.*

No. 330-S-3. Three light Pendant Fixture. Spread 16½ inches. Length 42 inches. *Price $10.50.*

Finish: Etruscan Gold

NOTE: No. 330-PL-1 and No. 330-S-1 also furnished in Ivory and Colors for Bedroom and Breakfast Room use. (See Page 48.)

Glass Shade: No. 24243
Champagne Satin Tone.

No. 330-C-3. Three light Ceiling Fixture. (Similar to 330-C-5). Spread 16½ inches. Length 11½ inches. *Price $10.50.*

No. 330-C-5. Five light Ceiling Fixture. Spread 19½ inches. Length 11½ inches. *Price $16.50.*

No. 330-S-5. Five light Pendant Fixture. Spread 19½ inches. Length 42 inches. *Price $16.50.*

Page 10

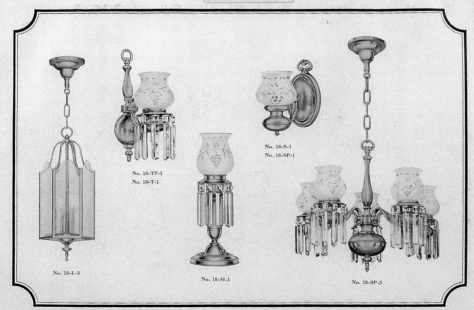

No. 18-TP-1
No. 18-T-1

No. 18-S-1
No. 18-SP-1

No. 18-L-3

No. 18-M-1

No. 18-SP-5

—necessary to properly complete an interior of this period.

Concord Series

No. 18-L-3. Three candle light Pendant Lantern. Spread 8½ inches. Length 36 inches. Removable clear glass panels. *Price $25.00.*

No. 18-TP-1. One light Wall Bracket. Backplate 4½x13½ inches. Covers 3-inch outlet. Extension 6 inches. Pull Chain Socket. Clear cut Colonial Shade No. 24218. Trimmed with wood-polished Colonial-cut prisms of the finest quality. *Price $15.00.*

No. 18-T-1. Same as No. 18-TP-1, except without Colonial-cut prisms. *Price $12.00.*

No. 18-M-1. One light Portable Mantle Torchere. Base Diameter 5½ inches. Height 14 inches. Canopy switch control. Equipped with 6 feet of cord and attachment plug. Clear cut Colonial Shade No. 24218. Wood-polished Colonial-cut prisms. *Price $9.00.*

Choice of Finishes: "Colonial Brass" or "Weathered Brass"

NOTE: All fixtures shown on this page sold complete with shades only.

No. 18-S-1. One light Wall Bracket. Backplate 4½x7½ inches. Covers 4-inch outlet. Extension 7 inches. Canopy switch control. Clear cut Colonial Shade No. 24218. *Price $10.50.*

No. 18-SP-1. Same as No. 18-S-1, except equipped with wood-polished Colonial-cut prisms. *Price $12.00.*

No. 18-SP-5. Five light Pendant Fixture. Spread 22 inches. Length 42 inches. Clear cut Colonial Shades No. 24218. Wood-polished Colonial-cut prisms. *Price $60.00.*

Page 14

Above: Art Deco style fixtures from the 1933 Moe Bridges Catalogue No. 35, Milwaukee, Wisconsin. Although similar fixtures are being reproduced, there is currently no source for replacement shades for this particular style. No. 330-PL-1: $45-$110; No. 330-S-1: $55-$125; No. 330-S-3: $95-$225; No. 330-C-5: $75-$175; No. 330-S-5: $145-$325.

Left: 1933 Moe Bridges fixtures in the Colonial style. No. 18-L-3: $50-$110; No. 18-TP-1: $100-$275; No. 18-M-1: $125-$200; No. 18-S-1: $70-$175; No. 18-SP-5: $275-$550.

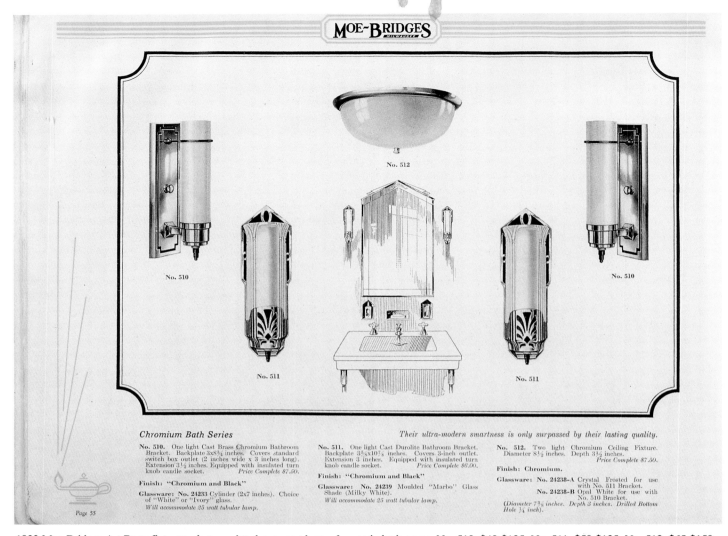

No. 512

No. 510

No. 510

No. 511

No. 511

Chromium Bath Series

Their ultra-modern smartness is only surpassed by their lasting quality.

No. 510. One light Cast Brass Chromium Bathroom Bracket. Backplate 3x8¾ inches. Covers standard switch box outlet (2 inches wide x 3 inches long). Extension 3½ inches. Equipped with insulated turn knob candle socket. *Price Complete $7.50.*

Finish: "Chromium and Black"

Glassware: No. 24233 Cylinder (2x7 inches). Choice of "White" or "Ivory" glass.
Will accommodate 25 watt tubular lamp.

No. 511. One light Cast Durolite Bathroom Bracket. Backplate 3⅝x10⅞ inches. Covers 3-inch outlet. Extension 3 inches. Equipped with insulated turn knob candle socket. *Price Complete $6.00.*

Finish: "Chromium and Black"

Glassware: No. 24239 Moulded "Marbo" Glass Shade (Milky White).
Will accommodate 25 watt tubular lamp.

No. 512. Two light Chromium Ceiling Fixture. Diameter 8½ inches. Depth 3½ inches. *Price Complete $7.50.*

Finish: Chromium.

Glassware: No. 24238-A Crystal Frosted for use with No. 511 Bracket. No. 24238-B Opal White for use with No. 510 Bracket. (Diameter 7⅜ inches. Depth 3 inches. Drilled Bottom Hole ¼ inch).

Page 55

1933 Moe Bridges Art Deco fixtures, chrome plated over cast brass; for use in bathrooms. No. 510: $40-$125; No. 511: $50-$135; No. 512: $65-$150.

Four radio lamps from the 1930s. Made of pot metal with a choice of finishes, these small figural lamps were decoratively placed on top of radio consoles during the 1930s and 40s. The period shades with 3 1/4" fitters are in some instances replacements, but they are all of the period. Heights range from 12 1/2" to 15 1/2" and bases from 4 1/2" to 7". $150-$375 each. *Courtesy of Samuel Furrer.*

100

Art glass lamp, circa 1925, features a hand blown orange and gold surface with applied thread design, possibly the work of the Durand Art Glass Company, located in Vineland, New Jersey and in operation from 1924 to 1931. Rewired with new socket and harp, this lamp measures 6" x 21". $275-$400. *Courtesy of Nadja Maril Historic Lighting.*

Opposite page:
Bottom right: Novelty lamp for providing light and displaying flowers. Designed for use on a sideboard or entry table, these lamps were marketed in the 1920s and 30s. Hand painted glass, brass and plating over base metal with some deterioration on the base, approximately 7" x 20". $65-$125. *Courtesy of Anita Mueller, Hico, Texas.*

Pair of art glass lamps, circa 1925. Gold aurene glass with gold leafed, wood carved mounts most likely the work of the Steuben Glass Works located in Corning New York and founded in 1902. Rewired with new sockets. 4 1/2" x 18". $400-$650 for the pair. *Courtesy of Nadja Maril Historic Lighting.*

Three lamps from the 1930s. The lamp on the far left, with original bronze finish, is in need of rewiring and takes some of its styling from an Argand Lamp, 15" x 22". $45-$90. The center lamp is made of alabaster, made to resemble an old vase from Greece or Rome. 7" x 20". $40-$90. *Courtesy of Esta Maril.* Lamp on the far right is a combination of polished brass and hammered copper and is rewired. One of a pair of lamps in the Arts and Crafts style, it measures 6" x 18". $150-$265 each. *Courtesy of Nadja Maril Historic Lighting.*

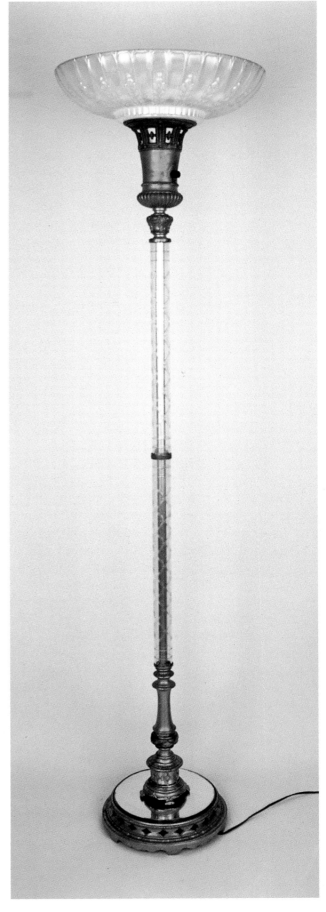

1930s torchiere lamp, rewired but otherwise all original. Cut glass, with interior metal support rod, gilded base metal, and mirrored base. Molded glass shade has sprayed iridescent finish. 12" x 66". $275-$450. *Collection of Nadja Maril.*

Chapter Five
A Primer on Metals

Identification

The first step in purchasing or restoring a lamp partially made of metal is to identify what type of metal it is.

Unless you have something made of iron or copper (which are elements), most metal lamps are made of alloys. In fact, one of the definitions of metal is, "A composition of some metallic element; also an alloy: generally with a qualifying word."

Some of the common alloys one encounters in the antique trade are **bronze, pewter, brass, white metal,** and **pot metal**. What distinguishes one from another is not just the elements used, but the proportions. Both white metal and brass are made from a combination of copper and zinc (brass was sometimes also made from copper and tin). Brass gets its reddish gold color from copper, whereas white metal looks white from the zinc.

One easy way to distinguish brass from other metals containing steel, nickel, or cobalt is to use a magnet. Sometimes an iron rod is used to give inside support or weight to an item such as a lamp or chandelier, so take that into consideration when judging whether or not the magnet is attracted to the metal being tested.

Bronze is an alloy of copper and tin, copper and aluminum, or sometimes copper and manganese. Once again, note that some early brass was also made of copper and tin, just in different proportions.

Over time, metals oxidize. Bronze often turns green. This process is called *verde antico*, and is sometimes done intentionally to new bronze by applying a solution of aromatic vinegar and sea salt. Brass gradually turns almost black, although I have also seen tinges of green; this greatly depends on the environmental factors. Bronze also tends to darken, but the process is slower and less dramatic than with brass.

Pewter is an alloy of tin and lead, while pot metal is a combination of copper and lead. Although some folks describe pot metal as having received its name from different pieces of old metal being thrown into a pot and melted down for re-use, the name was actually coined because it was the appropriate metal for constructing pots. Due to the softness of lead, pewter and pot metal are less durable alloys, and thus more susceptible to damage over time.

Broken metal composed of the more durable alloys can be repaired, but the repair will never entirely be invisible. Many pieces can be soldered together using lead solder and a blow torch. Plated metals whose finish has worn away need to be re-plated. Antiques of darkened bronze or brass need cleaning and possibly polishing.

As shown in the photographic illustrations, a variety of finishes were applied to metals, particularly brass. Many different shades of colors and many different textures were selected by lighting designers and artisans; these should be left as they are found. By removing the original finish you not only destroy a piece of the past, you also severely devalue your fixture.

Sometimes the best cleaning is simply mild soap and water. However, if you are dealing with a piece which was originally shiny and is now badly tarnished, it is possible to hand polish the piece using strong commercial polish and a very fine steel wool pad. After the initial polishing has been completed, the piece should be subsequently polished with a soft cloth. This method is good for items which are still recognizable as being brass or bronze.

For other items, one may want to employ the services of a professional polisher, who uses a dipping solution along with a buffing wheel to remove layers of dirt, paint, and lacquer. This can provide quick, effective results and is well worth the financial investment. In order to polish a piece on a buffing wheel, the piece is completely taken apart. If a protective coating of lacquer is desired, the lacquer is applied to each separate piece before they are reassembled.

The buffing wheel used by professional polishers holds a piece of soft cotton or muslin, which applies a polishing compound to remove tarnish from the metal's surface. The compound is made up of three different components: an abrasive (usually silicon, emery, or iron oxide), an adhesive, and an inert substance such as wax.

Three types of shines can be achieved when a piece is polished by a professional on a buffing wheel: 1) a traditional bright polish 2) an antique polish in which the evenness and brightness is toned down, and 3) a satin finish, which uses a coarser abrasive to provide a soft finish.

Many beautiful pieces of metal were created with a unique finish, consisting of a plating which was then treated with acid or chemicals. Good examples of this are the lamps of Philip Handel made in Meriden, Connecticut in the late nineteenth and early twentieth century. Handel lamp bases, which are highly prized, were made of white metal with a coating of copper. This coating was then specially treated to create such finishes as verde green, red copper, and English bronze. In order to repatinate such pieces if the finish has worn off, the piece must first be re-plated with copper.

Sometime an original finish is inadvertently removed by an overzealous polisher. Before polishing, therefore, it is important to first ascertain what kind of metal you are dealing with and research how the piece originally looked.

Care and Protection

If the lamp was meant to look shiny, the question often posed is: "How can I make that shine last?" A special patinated finish might also warrant a protective coating. There are several schools of thought regarding what should be used to protect brass and various colored finishes on metal.

Many advocate the use of lacquer, which protects a piece from both wear and the environment. A lacquered piece is never polished, and thus the metal is less likely to deteriorate from polish residue used in cleaning which becomes left in the cracks.

Lacquer, however, is not permanent. It lasts five to eight years depending on environmental conditions and may discolor over time. Extremes of temperature, salt, moisture, ultra violet light, and air pollution all contribute to the deterioration of a lacquered surface.

The protective alternative to lacquer is wax. Wax can either be applied directly to the brass in thin coats twenty four hours apart, or applied on top of lacquer for double protection. Wax should not be applied to a freshly lacquered piece. The lacquer first needs time to cure.

When ready, apply a small amount of wax (about the size of a nickel) with a soft rag. Initially the wax appears an opaque white, but as it is spread and buffed into the metal it will disappear.

Application of wax directly onto metal will slow oxidation and allow a glowing patina to gradually develop. On a lacquered surface, wax can provide a flexible seal to help protect the surface should the different expansion rates of the metal and lacquer cause lifting or cracking.

Lamps which are frequently handled are likely to develop holes or scratches in a lacquered finish, which will then accelerate tarnishing beneath the surface. As a stop gap method, the tarnishing process can be delayed by first cleaning the surface grit from the affected area with very fine steel wool and then polishing it back up to the desired shine. Carefully dry the metal both inside and out (a hair dryer set on a low temperature can be used), because more porous metals can trap water which will lead to internal corrosion. Finally, apply a thin coat of wax. If you know what kind of lacquer was used (water based or alcohol based), you could also apply spray lacquer to the area rather than wax.

What type of wax should you use to protect brass, copper, silver plate, or other metals? There is a product on the market specifically called Brass Wax. Other products called Butcher's Wax and Bee's Wax are available as well. You want to select a wax which has no added color and is microcrystalline in structure. Microcrystalline wax is any wax which retains its crystal structure, even under the microscope. The crystals are an essential component in creating a protective barrier between the metal's surface and the outside elements.

A third option is to keep your metal "natural" without a protective coating. The rate at which various metals tarnish depends on many factors, including moisture in the air, pollution, dirt, soot, and the amount of physical contact.

The proximity of brass or copper to fresh paint or to chemical cleaning agents will greatly accelerate the tarnishing process and/or deteriorate any protective coatings placed on the metal's surface. Strong carpet shampoos as well as ammonia products used to clean windows and mirrors can all cause damage to nearby metal lighting fixtures. If possible, move lighting fixtures out of areas where major cleaning or painting operations are taking place. Otherwise, make certain all lighting fixtures are adequately protected.

Gloves should be worn when a fixture is being installed. The gloves will prevent fingerprints from appearing on unprotected brass, and will protect a lacquered surface from scratches. Keys and gemstones on rings can create permanent scratches on metal surfaces. Handle pieces carefully and always keep them well supported.

Metals and water do not generally mix. Brass fixtures installed in damp areas, such as bathrooms and kitchens, deteriorate quickly, whether or not they are protected with a coating. A combination of lacquer and wax is probably the best choice for those who want to keep their fixtures shiny and bright. The other choice is to do a touch up polish on a piece every two to three weeks and a complete polishing approximately every six months.

Cleaning

The first step to polishing a piece is cleaning it. Always remove the shades from a lamp or fixture so they will not get damaged in the cleaning process. Grease and dirt should be removed with a dust cloth or a damp cloth. A very dirty surface will need to be washed with soapy water. Use a mild non-ionic emollient type of cleaner such as Ivory dishwashing liquid. Do not use ammonia or alcohol based cleaners.

Make certain your lamp base or fixture is completely dry before you proceed. Use a soft cloth to soak up any moisture which may have become trapped in cracks or crevices.

Apply a quality polish, following the directions, and buff thoroughly. Make certain the polish is completely removed when you are finished. If you leave any polish residue behind, it will continue to eat into the metal's surface and cause deterioration.

Lacquered pieces that become greasy or dirty need to be periodically cleaned using the above mentioned cleaning method. Never try to polish a lacquered piece, unless you are touching up an area where the lacquer seal was broken, as described earlier in this chapter.

Bronze fixtures and lamps with various plated and patinated finishes need periodic cleaning as well, but the cleaning should always be as non-intrusive as possible. Never use a hard brush or strong chemicals. Dust regularly with a soft cloth or special dusting brush. Remove dirt with a non-ionic soap solution applied with a sponge, soft cloth, or soft brush. Dry the metal thoroughly with a soft absorbent cloth. A light application of wax, buffed well, will protect the finish and add some shine.

Damage

A lot of stresses over time can occur to metals which are alloys. One common occurrence which takes place in brass is called de-zincification. It is characterized by pitting on the metal's surface. Since brass is often a combination of copper and zinc, the zinc gets eaten away faster by repeated polishing and the surface then turns pink from the predominance of copper.

This type of discoloration is common in fixtures over seventy-five years old. There is nothing that can be done to correct the variation in color, and many collectors feel it adds character to a piece. A minor amount of discoloration may be helpful in quickly distinguishing an older piece from a reproduction.

Pieces made of brass that was flattened, beaten, hammered, and shaped into forms to create the various components for fixtures are not as durable as brass which was cast. Copper is more malleable than zinc, so pieces for molding contain more copper to give them flexibility. These "flexible" pieces are the ones which crack, split, and break. They are thin, and when repeatedly stressed they give way.

If you need to bend a piece back into position, do so gently. It can and will break. Cracks and breaks can be soldered, but scars will remain.

A common area where a piece will fall apart is the shade holder. The heat from the gas jet or light bulb, as well as the activity of screwing or unscrewing a shade, will cause splits in the shade holder. To further compound this problem, the threading for the screws will fall out. In order to repair the shade holder, the screw holes need to be drilled and threaded.

Commonly, many people simply replace the damaged shade holder with another, rather than spending the time and money on repairs. This is a value judgment that should be made using the following criteria: 1) Are the shade holders unique to the fixture? 2) Are the shade holders signed or do they have some other important historical documentation? 3) Do I have other shade holders similar in configuration of approximately the same age?

To replace broken or missing cast components, molds can be made by a professional who works with metal restoration. The piece is reattached by soldering. Plating a piece adds another layer of reinforcement and thus may be helpful in solidifying repairs.

Gluing is a last resort for metal repairs. If all else fails, the best type of glue to use is two part epoxy which you mix together before using.

The common adage when repairing any antique or collectible piece is to do as little as possible with as few changes as possible.

A selection of gas brackets representing both the different styles of the late nineteenth century as well as the wide variety of original finishes which can be found on the metal surfaces of old lighting fixtures. These examples are primarily from the Gaslight Collection of Dan and Nancy Mattausch. They are all in their original finish and have not been treated with anything harsher than soap and water. While all these brackets are solid brass, polishing would destroy their original appearance.

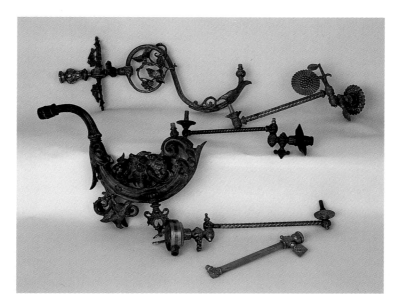

Clockwise from left:
1) Rococo revival style bracket from the 1860s. Heavy cast ornamentation includes grapes, morning glories and lilies. Burnishing and an acid wash were probably used to achieve the gold finish on the brass. $150-$350.
2) High Victorian style bracket from the 1880s with grape and morning glory leaves. The brass has a yellow/green color. $150-$275.
3) Influenced by the style of William Morris, this sunflower bracket from the turn of the century has its original back plate and drip cup. It was acid treated and lacquered to appear like copper. $75-$135.
4) Made between 1870 and 1890, with its original back plate and drip cup, this bracket has a bronze finish accented with gold colored highlights. $35-$85.
5) Cornelius and Baker, circa 1860, with original drip cup. This bracket uses the burnished and matte finishes as part of its ornamentation. The original box back plate is very unusual and rare in this time period. This type of back plate was used when gas was retrofitted in a building by putting the pipes directly on the interior walls. $75-$150.
6) Nickel plated bracket, made between 1880 and 1900 with geometric ornamentation; most commonly used in bathrooms and kitchens. $25-$65.

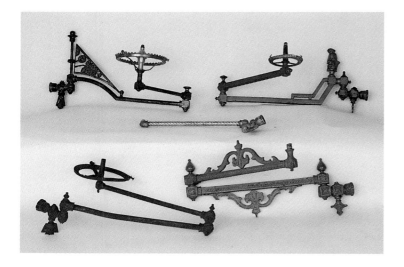

From top left, moving clockwise:
1) Circa 1880 double swing arm bracket by Thackara Sons & Co. in the style of the Aesthetic movement, with empire burner and scallop 4" fitter. The finish is highly polished, acid washed, and lacquered with a copper tint. $110-$210.
2) Pre-1870 double arm swing bracket, painted coating over brass with figural decoration and a cast fitter for a 2 5/8" shade. $125-$225.
3) Single swing arm brass bracket from the early 1900s with gold toned finish. $20-$48.
4) Double swing Renaissance Revival style bracket, Number 1418 in the Mitchell, Vance and Company Catalogue of 1876. Heavy brass with an orange colored finish. $100-$200.
5) Double brass swing arm bracket "in the rough," 1890-1920 with fitter for 4" shade. What constituted the original finish on this particular bracket, no one knows. While some type of restoration would be necessary if this piece is to be used and enjoyed, bright polishing would not be a historically accurate approach. $15-$45.

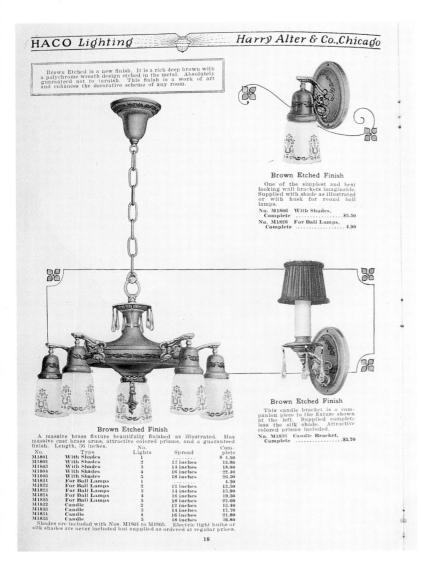

HACO Lighting   Harry Alter & Co., Chicago

Brown Etched is a new finish. It is a rich deep brown with a polychrome wreath design etched in the metal. Absolutely guaranteed not to tarnish. This finish is a work of art and enhances the decorative scheme of any room.

Brown Etched Finish

One of the simplest and best looking wall brackets imaginable. Supplied with shade as illustrated or with husk for round ball lamps.

No. M1806 With Shades,
    Complete $5.50
No. M1826 For Ball Lamps,
    Complete 4.90

Brown Etched Finish

This candle bracket is a companion piece to the fixture shown at the left. Supplied complete less the silk shade. Attractive colored prisms included.

No. M1836 Candle Bracket,
    Complete $5.70

Brown Etched Finish

A massive brass fixture beautifully finished as illustrated. Has massive cast brass arms, attractive colored prisms, and a guaranteed finish. Length, 36 inches.

No.	Type	No. Lights	Spread	Complete
M1801	With Shades	1	....	$ 4.50
M1802	With Shades	2	12 inches	13.80
M1803	With Shades	3	14 inches	18.06
M1804	With Shades	4	16 inches	22.40
M1805	With Shades	5	18 inches	26.50
M1821	For Ball Lamps	1	....	4.30
M1822	For Ball Lamps	2	12 inches	12.50
M1823	For Ball Lamps	3	14 inches	15.90
M1824	For Ball Lamps	4	16 inches	19.50
M1825	For Ball Lamps	5	18 inches	22.60
M1832	Candle	2	12 inches	13.40
M1833	Candle	3	14 inches	17.70
M1834	Candle	4	16 inches	21.80
M1835	Candle	5	18 inches	26.80

Shades are included with Nos. M1801 to M1805. Electric light bulbs or silk shades are never included but supplied as ordered at regular prices.

18

Fixtures advertised in the 1924 Haco Lighting Fixtures Catalogue "M", introducing Brown Etched, a deep brown finish with a polychrome wreath design etched in the metal.

Two 1920s pan fixtures "as found." In order for these fixtures to be correctly restored they cannot be polished or they will lose their decorative finish.

Reproduction versus original. When a copy is made from an original casting, some of the detail is lost. Although the castings on these pieces are not the same, the difference in quality between old and new is obvious.

Before and after. The electric wall bracket on the right has been stripped of paint, polished, and rewired while its mate has been left in original condition. They are shown with period signed Holophane shades. Early electric brackets circa 1905, they measure 8" x 7". $265-$325 for the restored pair. *Courtesy of Nadja Maril Historic Lighting.*

Close-up of the back of an electric wall bracket, showing a Miller signature, standing for the Edward Miller Company of Meriden, Connecticut.

Two brass pan fixtures. The one on the left has several layers of paint and the one on the right has been polished and rewired. Shown with molded period satin glass shades with interior and molded floral decoration, the right fixture measures 14" x 21". $195-$275. *Courtesy of Nadja Maril Historic Lighting.*

Two inverted gas and electric fixtures, copper plating over brass and steel. The one on the lower right with waffle pattern signed period Holophane shades has been carefully polished and lacquered and measures 29" x 40". The coloration of the finish was an "antique copper." If too much copper were to be buffed off, the fixture would become shiny brass. The fixture on the left is in its original "as found" condition. Restored with shades, $650-$1200. *Courtesy of Nadja Maril Historic Lighting.*

The lacquer seal on the base of this floor lamp has broken, enabling the brass to discolor in one area.

Pairpoint Puffy boudoir lamp. Also called a "Blown-Out," the yellow, pink, blue, and white decoration was painted and fired onto the inside of the shade. The bronze base is in mint condition. It has its original lacquer coating. Proper care is a light dusting. 6 1/2" x 11 1/2". $2800-$3700. *Courtesy of an anonymous collector.*

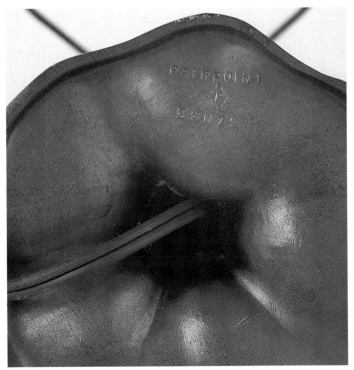

A close-up of the bottom of the tree trunk base shown in the previous picture, signed "Pairpoint Mfg. Co." and numbered B3979.

Chapter Six
Glass

Preventing Breakages

Old lamps and lighting fixtures often have glass shades. Glass breaks. Not only does glass break, it cracks, chips, and flakes. Part of the beauty of glass and our attraction to it as an art form is its fragility.

Philosophers often talk about the glass being half empty or half full. But let's think for a moment about the glass itself. At any moment, a strong wind, an earthquake, or the accidental sweep of one's arm may knock the glass over, causing it to fall and break. We all know the potential for breaking is there, which is why we value pieces of beautiful antique glass so highly.

An antique glass shade, just by being an antique, has already somehow survived over one hundred years without breaking. It's a miracle. Or is it?

The large shades made for reverse painted lamps were made of heavy glass, which could withstand being successively baked in kilns at temperatures as high as 800 degrees Fahrenheit so that various textures and decorations could be permanently adhered to the glass. The Handel Company of Meriden, Connecticut advertised that their glass lamps would last a lifetime. True to that promise, many of their lamps have easily survived to the present.

Most breakages to lamps occur when they are being moved and when they are in storage. The majority of damage to lamps probably takes place in the hands of dealers. Not that dealers are careless—they have a lot of money invested in each lamp. However, chips occur when lamps are banged into by careless customers, by falling displays, by accidents in transit, and by poor packing techniques.

The shades which go on brackets and hanging fixtures often become damaged for four reasons. Reason number one is that the three set screws which hold the shade in place are sometimes screwed in too tightly, causing the glass to fracture or chip. Since this damage is not seen once the shade is installed, it does not seriously detract from a shade's value within a multiple set of shades. If you have such a piece, rotate the shade when installing it in the shade holder so that the damaged section is not further subjected to contact with one of the three set screws. *Turn your set screws tightly enough to hold the shade in place, but not so tight as to put extra tension on the glass.* An installed light bulb will often prevent the shade from being knocked loose to the ground, even if the screws are jarred and let go.

Reason number two is that too large or high a wattage bulb is installed in the fixture. When the bulb makes physical contact with the shade, it will overheat that section of the glass, causing it to fracture and crack. *Always make certain there is at least one half inch of space between a glass shade and a light bulb.* Refrain from using wattages higher than seventy-five watts in small shades. It is infinitely safer to use forty or sixty watt bulbs.

There are many different sizes and shapes of light bulbs, available at stores specializing in lighting or home improvement, as well as at hardware stores. Small size clear appliance bulbs look similar to early bulbs (without the air bubble at the tip). Long tubular bulbs can be used for breadloaf shades. Bulbs shaped like a candle flame work well inside the electrified chimneys of old oil lamps.

Reason number three also has to do with heat and glass. In this instance, it is the rapid change from hot to cold. *Spray cold cleaning fluid on a hot glass shade and the glass will crack.* Only clean glass shades when they are at room temperature. Use warm water and mild soap as directed in Chapter Five. If you have outside persons coming into your home to clean, instruct them to stay away from your lamps.

Reason number four has to do with the chips and breaks which occur when someone's head or an object bangs into one of the shades installed in a hanging fixture, wall bracket, or table lamp. This type of damage is hard to predict or prevent. Generally, it is a good idea to place expensive lamps away from high traffic areas. A lamp placed on top of a high buffet in the dining room is much safer than one placed on a table in the entrance hall. If you are having a large party or meeting, move your expensive lamps to safe places. If pieces of furniture are being carried into your home or apartment, remove the shades on chandeliers before the movers arrive.

Never trust professional movers to pack your lamps and other fragile antiques. The majority of broken lamps which come to me for appraisals were packed by movers. Once you have carefully wrapped up your glass shades for shipping or transport, they can be safely moved by someone else. If you value something, pack it yourself.

There is an old saying, "an ounce of prevention is worth a pound of cure." This is definitely true when it comes to glass shaded lamps.

Repairing Broken Glass and Porcelain

So what do you do if a glass shade does break? If it breaks into a thousand small pieces you throw them in the trash can. However, if it breaks into two or three pieces you can try gluing them back together. Always use an epoxy. If you are not pleased with the results, the bond can be broken with acetone and the pieces reglued. If you use Super Glue the results are often permanent. Professionals in the field of antique restoration use an epoxy called Hxtal, which is as strong as glass. It takes eight to twelve hours to dry, however, and this long period of drying time is not always practical for keeping pieces correctly in place. Two part epoxy, available at most hardware stores and hobby shops, can provide an effective bond and dries in minutes.

Epoxy can also be used to repair pottery and china bases which break. Make certain the surface is clean. First wash with a non-ionic cleaner such as a mild dishwashing liquid, then wipe down with denatured alcohol to seal porous surfaces.

Take your time when doing a repair. Make certain the pieces are correctly positioned and balanced, so that they will stay in place. Small pieces of gum backed tape can be used as "band aids" to hold pieces in place.

A repaired piece can still be enjoyed. If the shade belongs on a chandelier, be careful to keep the wattage below sixty watts, as the glued shade will be more liable to develop heat damage.

A flake on the edge of a shade can often be successfully filed down by hand with an emery board. Using an emery board can also reduce the size of chips.

A professional glass repair person can help you with gluing a piece back together. He can also help if you wish to have the edges of a shade ground down on a wheel. Glass grinding works well on pieces of heavy glass, such as cut crystal, but can be risky on glass shades since these are made of thinner glass which can shatter and break under pressure. Also be aware that with a set of shades, you will now have made one shade shorter than the others.

It is inadvisable to have chips ground off the edge of reverse painted shades, if only because the signatures are usually located on the rim of the glass. Dealers who specialize in reverse painted lamps often fill chips in with a mixture of epoxy. The epoxy dries clear, whereas most shades were made of opal or frosted glass. A good repair artist will first mix color into the epoxy and then blend paint onto the shade that will match the existing background or decoration after it dries.

Leaded Glass and Panels with Metalwork

Lamp shades constructed from what is termed slag glass (referred to as Art glass during the era), opaque colored glass characterized by multiple striations, are usually held together in two basic ways. The various panels are either held in place by metal frames, often with tabs to hold them in place, or they are held together with bands of soldered lead.

For repairs to any of these types of lamps, a studio must first be located that specializes in the construction of new stained glass or leaded glass lighting fixtures. Often a hobby shop, which sells the supplies for stained glass construction, can help you locate such an artisan. A missing panel in a lamp held together with metalwork could be repaired by locating a matching piece of glass and having it cut to the appropriate size, as long as the panels are flat.

If you have a lamp with one or more missing curved glass panels, you will need to find an artisan equipped with a kiln. A mold is made of your lamp, and the panel is shaped and bent, with the assistance of the heated kiln, around the mold.

Leaded glass panels may need soldering, and/or portions of glass may need replacement. The matching of colors, texture, and solder is very important. It is better to wait until you locate the appropriate supplies then to go ahead and fix a lamp with the wrong pieces of glass.

Spotting Repairs

You can spot chips which have been filled by carefully feeling the edges of the shade. On a painted shade, a repaired spot will usually include the application of new paint designed to distract the eye. Closely examine the painting on a painted shade for any variations. If you suspect repairs have been made to a lamp you can also use a black light to further inspect the piece.

A black light is a tool used by museum conservators and appraisers which emits long wave ultraviolet radiation invisible to the human eye. The ultraviolet radiation is absorbed by the electrons on the surface of the china or glass and causes them to move and then be replaced by other electrons. This activity is called fluorescence. Fluorescent light is visible to the human eye.

Old materials fluoresce differently from new materials. Therefore, recently painted or repaired areas will react differently and will look different from the original surfaces. When you examine a piece with a black light, you are not looking for a particular fluorescent color but for *differences* in color.

Replacement Shades

If a glass shade is broken or missing, the only option is replacement. Ideally, the best replacement is with an old shade of the same approximate age, size, and design. Old glass shades for kerosene lamps and large diameter glass shades for table lamps are hard to find. There are so many more fixtures minus shades than shades themselves. When dealers do locate an old shade, they usually save it to match up with the appropriate lamp. It is possible to find an orphaned 7" antique student lamp shade—anything is possible—but it is not probable.

On the other hand, there are plenty of old standard 2 1/4" fitter shades for electric fixtures. (I have hundreds in my basement.) It is difficult to find sets of three or more old matching electric shades with acid etched decoration because they are so popular.

The situation with gas shades, 4" and 5" fitters, lies somewhere in the middle. Antique pattern glass shades for old gas fixtures can be located, but acid etched gas shades are becoming increasingly rare. There are many singles but very few sets of old gas acid etched shades currently on the market.

If you are looking for a replacement shade, you need to furnish the correct dimensions when contacting dealers and suppliers. The fitter size of a shade is the part which rests or screws into a fixture or lamp. The fitter size of an electric shade is the smaller opening which is attached with the three set screws. The fitter size of a chimney is the width of the opening which sits in the holder.

The other important dimensions are the entire diameter of the shade at its widest point and its height. This gives the dealer or supplier the information they need to check on what they may have available.

Reproduction shades for gas or electric style lights are being made in the following fitter sizes: 2 1/4", 2 5/8", 3 1/4", and 4". Reproduction kerosene lamp shades are available for 4", 7", 10", 12", and 14" size fitters. There are replacement shades for torchieres made in 2 1/4", 2 3/4", and 3 1/4" fitter sizes, as well as replacement shades for early twentieth century electric fixtures with 4", 6", and 12" openings. Angle Lamp glass shades with 3 1/4" bottom fitters and a 5 1/2" chimney fitter, are also being reproduced.

The best reproduction shades are those which most closely mimic the look and feel of original shades. The easiest way to imitate the real thing is to use the same production techniques. Shades which are hand blown and hand cut on a wheel are superior to those which are poured into molds by machine. However, much of the quality standards in glass production have deteriorated over the years. The final judge of quality is you, the consumer.

The best place to look at what is currently being made is at new lighting stores and gift shops. If you look at the reproductions first in context, they will be much easier to spot in antique shops and at antique shows. Never assume something is old just because it is being sold by an antique dealer.

Marriages

In the antique trade, "marriage" is a term used to describe two pieces which have been joined together. The bookcase top of a secretary might be removed because it was too tall to fit into a particular room. Later that top might be sold separately and put together with the desk portion of another secretary. The woods might be the same but the proportions different. An astute collector will notice the piece is "not quite right" and value it accordingly.

In the world of lamps, advances in lighting technology meant that lamps were constantly being improved and styles were changed. Oil burners were replaced with more efficient oil burners. Later, the burners were removed or cut apart for electrification. Glass shades were replaced by parchment and silk shades. Fixtures for gas were electrified. Electric fixtures first had exposed bulbs, then glass shades, and then it was back to exposed bulbs. Subsequently, glass shades were replaced by silk, parchment, and paper shades.

All these changes meant that many pieces were discarded. Some were saved in barns, attics, and basements. Collecting odd pieces with the intent of combining them with other orphans to make complete lamps can be an exciting and profitable enterprise. Unfortunately many pieces have been incorrectly joined together to make interesting "custom" lamps, which have little or no antique value.

It is important to remember that unless the two or more orphans are exact replacements of the pieces that preceded them, the value is less than an original piece. In certain instances, however, two pieces when married can dramatically increase in value. This situation is particularly applicable when talking about Reverse Painted table lamps.

For instance, a collector buys a beautiful silver-plated table lamp base for $300 made by the Pairpoint Manufacturing Company, once located in New Bedford, Massachusetts. He then finds an attractive reverse painted shade with a scenic design the appropriate size priced at $950 and buys it for the lamp. The shade, however, based on its shape and decoration, was most likely made by the Pittsburgh Brass, Glass and Lamp Company. By combining the shade and lamp together, the collector now has a lamp he can use and enjoy, costing him $1250 and worth approximately $1700. The Pairpoint base with a scenic Pairpoint shade, however, would be worth more.

The story continues... a few years later the same collector purchases a Pairpoint lamp with both signed base and shade. The owner sells it to him for $3300 because the finish on the base is damaged. He looks in a book on Pairpoints and sees his silver-plated base shown with the Pairpoint shade on the lamp he just purchased. He switches shades and increases the value of his new acquisition to $4000. His married lamp consisting of the damaged Pairpoint base and Pittsburgh Brass, Glass and Lamp Base is just slightly devalued to $1500 because of the less desirable base.

Because the silver-plated base is documented as being appropriate for the signed Pairpoint shade, the collector could safely put the two pieces together and actually increase the value over and above the value of the original Pairpoint lamp. It happens all the time. Dealers who specialize in Pairpoints, Handels, and other valuable reverse painted lamps are switching bases and shades constantly. Their chief motivating factor is monetary return.

Collectors, on the other hand, are concerned with the overall condition of a piece and the aesthetics. Often they fall in love with a particular style base and a certain shade. They want to buy that combination. Regardless of whether those exact pieces sold together in a store, if they saw the two together in a book or in someone else's collection, that is the lamp they want to purchase.

History buffs like me, as well as the curators of museums and historical buildings, are interested in keeping original pieces together whenever practical.

A certain amount of mixing and matching is inevitable in the lamp business. Various individuals have different agendas when it comes to purchasing lamps. The collector wants unusual examples. The curator of an historic building wants a piece which closely resembles what was actually used in the room. The dealer is looking for a lamp she can sell at a profit.

Marrying appropriate items together is important in maintaining value. Changes should be noted and communicated to the buyer. Unfortunately, antique lamps usually go through many hands before they find a home. The seller may therefore be unaware of previous changes to a lamp.

As a buyer, look at the lamp, wall bracket, or hanging fixture. Are the dimensions appropriate? Does the fitter cap (holding the shade in place) on a table lamp match the base? If it has been changed, it is likely the shade has been changed as well.

Cleaning Glass Shades

Etched glass, pattern glass, and art glass shades can be safely washed with warm water and gentle soap. A toothbrush can be used as an aid in loosening dirt which has solidified into crevices of the shade's design. Avoid dramatic changes in water temperature.

Use a dab of turpentine to remove stray paint flakes. Then rinse and wash afterwards, as previously directed.

Painted shades should always be tested before washing. If the color was baked onto the glass it is permanent. However, some shades were painted with colors which either fade or completely flake off with water contact.

I learned the hard way that not all reverse painted lamps have "permanent decoration." An unidentified reverse painted shade was in a box in my garage that was invaded by an opossum taking refuge from the cold winter. Quickly cleaning the inside of the shade with a garden hose, I realized too late that all the paint was coming off as well! This particular lamp had an inner coating of paint applied after the interior decoration, as a "fixative." Neither the coating nor the paint was *waterfast*. If you have a shade of this type, never wash it. The outside of the shade was meant to be simply dusted or wiped with a damp rag.

Leaded glass shades should be cleaned carefully. Strong cleaning agents will mar the finish of the leading. A small amount of turpentine on a cotton swab can be applied to soften hardened encrustation's. Immediately follow up by washing with warm soapy water using a firm fiber or nylon brush for cleaning dirt from crevices. A small amount of lemon oil can be applied to the glass after it is completely dry, to add some luster which may have faded with time. Do not use too much oil or it will act as a magnet for dust. Finally, wipe the shade dry with a soft lint-free cloth.

This close-up of a reverse painted Pairpoint 15" Carlisle shade shows the artist's signature, "W. Macy," which was painted on the inside of the glass shade at the same time this scene, known as "The Garden of Allah", was painted. "Pairpoint Corporation" was stamped on the opposite inside edge of the shade. Approximately ninety years old, this particular shade is in excellent condition. Entire lamp $3500-$4700. *Collection of Justin M. Patrick.*

Above: Early gas shades with 2 5/8"
fitter size (Note: These shades
were hand blown and have a very
pronounced lip. They are
sometimes confused with a 2 1/4"
electric shade). Top row, left to
right: Copper wheel engraved
wreath pattern, oval cut border
pattern along with frosted bands.
$45-$75; Greek key pattern with
frosted lower band and crimped
edge, circa 1860s. $45-$75.
Bottom row, left to right:
Cranberry frosted glass going to
clear with ruffled edge. $65-$125;
Copper wheel engraved floral
wreath pattern with large oval
border. $45-$75. Regarding shade
prices: antique shades are always
more valuable in sets. The larger
the set, the higher the value of
each shade.

Right: Gallery shades, 1 7/8" fitter
size. Top: Frosted glass with acid
etched torch and wreath design.
$20-$45. Second row, left to right:
Clear and frosted molded glass
octagon. $15-$40; Clear glass
with acid etched torch and wreath
design sitting in gallery burner.
$20-$45;
"Q" shade of white opal glass, has
air holes for galleries with no
bottom airflow. $10-$35.

Inverted gas shades with 3 1/4" fitter size. Top: Red frosted glass in the shape of a bunch of grapes; note air holes. Shown with Welsbach No. 6 Reflex brass burner. $50-$125. Second row, left to right: Green frosted glass in a similar design. $45-$120; Clear and frosted round shade on Welsbach No. 6 Reflex burner "in the rough." $8-$35; Satin glass shade of molded glass with colored flowers. $15-$45; Nickel plated Welsbach No.4 reflex burner with matching white opal 1 1/4" fitter globe. $10-$35; Frosted shade, acid etched design using a border stencil. $22-$60.

Gas and electric combination shades: 4" gas shades and 2 1/4" electric shades. Top row: set of green to clear frosted shades with ruffled edges decorated with an acid etched floral motif. $175-$250 for set. Bottom row, left to right: Set of white swirl opalescent Phoenix Glass Company hand blown shades with crimped edges. $145-$225 for set; Set of opaline shades with scalloped edges. $155-$235 for set. *Courtesy of the Gaslight Collection of Dan and Nancy Mattausch.*

Gas shades with 5" fitters on the top row. Left to right: Phoenix glass Company shade, acid etched with a basket weave and morning glory design. $85-$140; Hand blown opalescent hobnail shade. $120-$175. Gas shades with 4" fitters on the bottom row. Left to right: Opalescent quilt pattern hand blown shade. $110-$165; Crown shade with acid etched Anglo Japanese design. $90-$145; Frosted molded glass shade with acid etched ornamentation. $60-$95.

Four pattern glass 4" fitter shades in unusual patterns. $48-$85 each.

Below: A variety of textures are shown in these 2 1/4" shades, circa 1900-1920. Top row, left to right: Basket weave with blue border molded glass. $65-$140; Iridescent carnival glass with acid etched design of draped tassels and urns. $30-$60; Iridescent carnival glass with deep acid etched design of acorns and leaves. $35-$65. Front row, left to right: Two-tone satin glass. $65-$140; Crackle glass. $40-$90; Ripple glass. $40-$90.

2 1/4" shades, circa 1900-1930. Top row, left to right: Cased glass. $25-$45; Bisque fired. $15-$25; Interior decoration on molded glass. $5-$20; Signed frosted Holophane. $20-$50. Bottom row, left to right: Colored acid etched. $48-$120; Opalescent swirl. $48-$85; Frosted two-tone cranberry. $50-$125; Crackle glass with hand painted decoration. $25-$48.

Pages 124 & 125: Art glass shades, circa 1910-1930, with 2 1/4" fitters. Back row by Steuben Glass Works, left to right: $85-$135; $275-$400; $100-$150; $100-$150. Front row by the Quezel Art Glass Studio of New York; the first three shades are signed. Left to right: $85-$135; $110-$175; $85-$135; $100-$150.

Rolltop desk or cabinet top lamp with silhouette pattern in metal and blue slag glass shade. Circa 1920, the glass is held in place by metal tabs. Brass and iron with original ivorene finish and pull chain socket. 15" x 6" x 8". $325-$525.
Courtesy of Nadja Maril Historic Lighting.

Opposite page:
An example of a lamp marriage: signed Handel Base with bronze finish, 8" x 22", and 14" diameter cased green glass ice chip shade, both circa 1915. The Handel foundry opened in 1902. It did supply bases to other decorating workshops, so it is conceivable that this shade and lamp base, or ones similar to them, were sold together during the era. The shade may have been made in Germany for the McFaddin Company, which marketed Emeralites. $985-$1600.
Courtesy of Nadja Maril Historic Lighting.

THREE CHARMING BOUDOIR LAMPS

This attractive design is furnished with a richly colored scenic shade, harmonizing with the pink and white stand. Lamp is 14 inches high; shade, 8 inches in diameter. 1 light, push through socket.

No. M2410 Complete $6.50

The old ivory stand and handsome scenic shade make this lamp unusually graceful. It stands 14 inches high, and the shade is 8½ inches in diameter. 1 light, with push through socket; 2-piece plug.

No. M2411 Complete $7.00

An especially dainty model with blue shade containing a small floral design. Stand is white and blue. This lamp is 14 inches high, the shade 8 inches in diameter. 1 light; push through socket.

No. M2412 Complete $5.90

YOUR CHOICE OF THREE SHADES
ON THIS BEAUTIFUL TABLE LAMP

This attractive design depicts an old mill and pond. It is supplied with the Egyptian Bronze stand shown in the center. The shade is 16 inches in diameter, height of lamp complete is 22 inches. 2 lights, pull chain sockets and 2-piece plug.

No. M2413 Complete ...$23.50

This artistic table lamp consists of an Egyptian Bronze stand with delightfully-colored scenic shade. If desired, either of the shades illustrated on the right and left may be substituted. The lamp is 22 inches in height, and the shade 16 inches in diameter. 2 lights, equipped with pull chain sockets and 2-piece plug.

No. M2414 Complete $23.50

The shade contains a pastoral scene in deep, warm tones. It is supplied with the Egyptian Bronze stand illustrated in center. Shade is 16 inches in diameter, height of lamp 22 inches. 2 lights; pull chain sockets; 2-piece plug.

No. M2415 Complete ...$23.50

Circa 1860 gas pendant of cast iron with original (albeit worn) bronze and black polychrome finish made by the Tucker Manufacturing Company, 36 1/2" tall and 14" wide. The glassware, which uses both transfer and hand painted decoration, was found in two different places but perfectly match each other and the era in which the fixture was made. The gas shade fitter size is the early 2 5/8". $600-$950. *Courtesy of The Gaslight Collection of Dan and Nancy Mattausch.*

Opposite page:
This catalogue page, showing the same base with three different shade choices, indicates that it is possible to mix and match shades and bases in certain instances within the same time period. From the 1924 Haco Lighting Fixtures Catalog "M".

A variety of older shade holders for kerosene, gas, and early electric fixtures in many shapes and sizes. Sometimes available in junk boxes at flea markets for one to two dollars apiece, they can be worth as much as fifteen or twenty dollars to a collector trying to complete a lamp restoration.

Can you tell the reproduction from the original? The clarity of the molded design on the shade in the top row is superior. That's because it was made from the original mold, whereas its copy was made from a mold of an old shade.

Notice the clarity of the real Holophane shade on the top shelf when compared to its copy below. Reproduction Holophanes generally have a frosted lip and heavier weight. Two period acid etched shades are also on the top shelf. Below them is a reproduction shade which is lighter in weight. The etched decoration is not as sharp and the edges of the glass are rough. (Some acid etched reproduction shades are heavier than the originals; it depends on the design.)

Chapter Seven
Using Antique Lighting in Your Home

If you are a purist, you will keep a lamp as you originally found it and/or try to restore it back to its original condition. If your old lamp was meant to be used with oil or gas, you will not change it.

However, a practical person can just as easily argue, "I want to use my lamp and electricity is the power I use."

Old kerosene and old gas lamps can be safely used with their original fuels. It is your choice. Some of the supplies you need for using kerosene can be obtained by trading and buying parts from other collectors and dealers. New pieces can be ordered from lighting stores as well as found at rural hardware and marine supply stores.

You will have to be more enterprising if you wish to use gas, aggressively searching for old gas parts still in serviceable order. In order for a fixture to be used for gas it must not have been drilled for electrification, otherwise the piece needs to be resealed. The valves of old gas fixtures should be cleaned, lubricated, and checked for leaks. Plumber's putty can assist in sealing the joints.

For safety reasons, it is very important that you have your gas fixtures inspected by a professional before you attempt to hook them up for operation. A plumber can check for leaks in the pipes and a representative of the Gas and Electric Company can do an on site inspection. For more guidance, contact some of the resources listed at the back of this book.

If your choice is electrification, be as non-intrusive as possible. **Do not drill through a lamp.** Save old burners. There are units you can purchase which enable you to replace kerosene burners with electric ones, thus allowing you to use the original chimney and shade.

Electrifying gas lamps and fixtures sometimes means drilling the tubes originally used for gas to enlarge them to accommodate a standard electrical cord. When you electrify, try to maintain the components which hold the shades and chimneys. You may elect to use a smaller size light bulb socket, depending on the situation.

Rewiring and Restoration of Electric Lamps and Fixtures

I am not an electrician and therefore I strongly recommend that if you have concerns as to the safety of an electrified or electric lamp or fixture, you consult a professional.

If you feel comfortable doing your own rewiring, there are several books devoted specifically to wiring, which can take you through the process step by step. An added safety measure is to plug any questionable lamp into a separate circuit breaker strip available at the hardware store. If there is a wiring problem, the only fuse the fixture will blow is on the circuit breaker strip, which will then immediately turn itself off. Never touch or handle any exposed wires while a lamp is turned on.

If a fifty year old electric lamp is found perfectly preserved in its original box, does it need to be rewired? I would say no. The big error generally made with old electric lamps is an eagerness to replace all electric components in the interests of safety.

Frayed and exposed wires do need to be replaced. The brass shells of old electric sockets (often with their original patent dates) as well as old pull chains and Bakelite turn switches embossed with the initials of their maker are valuable artifacts which help document a lamp's age and history. They should be preserved and reused whenever possible. If you take a lamp to be rewired by someone else, make certain they reuse these pieces.

It is easier to put brand new pieces into a lamp than it is to recycle old components. Thus it is common to find new aluminum sockets on a beautiful old fixture. Quality replacement parts are available, which include brass socket covers, square turn switches, and silk covered cord.

Most dealers replace old wiring as a safety and sales feature.

Circa 1870 kerosene lamp, electrified in the 1920s. Although the burner was not saved, this lamp was correctly electrified without drilling and the original shade and chimney were kept. The decoupage decoration on the bottom of the glass base has deteriorated. 5" x 24". $285-$400. *Courtesy of Nadja Maril Historic Lighting.*

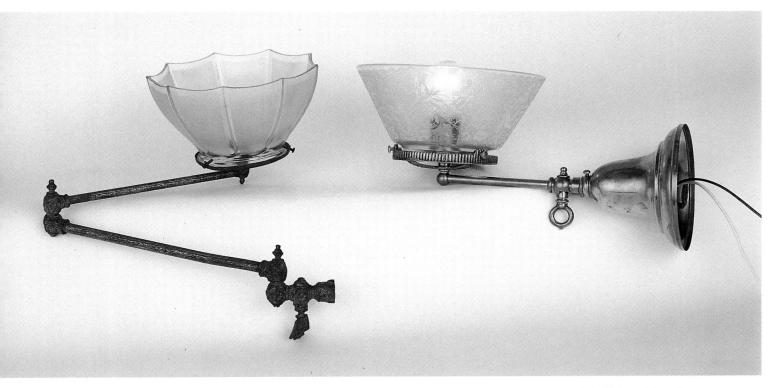

Two gas brackets with period shades, circa 1900. The double swing arm on the left is "in the rough" with its original 4" fitter shade holder and extends out 25". Shown with period octagonal frosted shade, with some careful restoration it could be used with gas. $135-$70. The bracket on the right, 5" x 11" with period acid etched shade, has been polished, lacquered, and electrified. A large canopy has been added to enable it to be attached to an electric box in the wall. $210-$325. *Courtesy of Nadja Maril Historic Lighting.*

Opposite page:
Electrified burning fluid lamp, circa 1850, with scallop shell pattern glass font, brass stem, and milk glass base, 4 1/2" x 10 1/2". The burner on this lamp has been removed and replaced with an electric socket and is shown with a new traditional paper shade. The lamp has not been drilled, and if the burner has been saved, it can be replaced at any time. $250-$350. *Courtesy of Ron Snyder Antiques, Annapolis, Maryland.*

The mate to the 1920s Regency Revival sconce on the right has been pulled apart for rewiring. Use of a vacuum cleaner and some string can help pull the new wire through the narrow holes. Make a diagram of the pieces when you take something apart, in order to help you remember how to put it back together.

A pair of 1920s brass lamps with original antique gold finish, 4" x 17". The lamp on the left has its original wiring which includes a small socket, appropriate for the original closed globe which has no bottom openings for air. The new, larger size socket could create too much heat for the shade. $245-$375 for the pair. *Courtesy of Nadja Maril Historic Lighting.*

Chapter Eight
Tips on Buying and Selling

A reader contacted me from Portland, Maine and asked me if I had some general advice for someone starting out in the antique lighting business.

I told him, "Always buy the best, because you will never have a problem selling quality pieces."

"But," he responded, "Being located up in Maine, I just can't seem to find anything that good."

I've done some of my best buying in Maine, I thought to myself, both from pickers and at auction. Why can't this gentleman find anything?

"Maybe you've already bought everything up," my husband told me jokingly.

But I knew that simply wasn't true. Antiques are constantly being unearthed, particularly when a market has developed.

You have to have the patience and desire to search the pieces down. Look everywhere: yard sales, flea markets, auctions, consignment shops, antique shows, and antique shops—even so called high priced antique shops. Not everyone knows the value of every item they are selling. Bargains can be found everywhere. Let folks know what you are looking for. Advertise. Leave your card.

One reason some collectors and dealers prefer *not* to advertise is their concern that prices will go up. Prices may initially rise. But as more pieces appear, the tendency will be for prices to decrease and then stabilize, based on supply and demand.

The greatest enemy of the antique lighting market is the quantity of reproductions. There are some beautiful quality reproductions being made, and there are situations when reproductions may be the only available choice. An eighteenth century building, for example, may need historically appropriate lighting and no antique fixtures can be located. A restaurant with a limited budget may be seeking twenty-five matching wall sconces in the gas and electric style. There is a need for reproductions, but as a result of their proliferation many home restorers have stopped buying original fixtures. The value of the original fixtures, in some instances, has consequently gone down.

Part of the problem is that when customers are insecure about what they are buying, they want to pay less. With all the reproductions, customers also become confused about what is old and what is new. This is why it is so important to retain as many original components as possible on an old lamp or fixture. Showing people dates, signatures, and written material about the piece can help make a sale.

If you are the buyer, ask for as much documentation as possible. If you are making a major purchase, ask for a written receipt with a description of what you are buying and inquire what type of guarantee the dealer is willing to offer. Even dealers can be fooled.

Approximately twelve years ago, a dealer sold me a scenic reverse painted lamp which was a signed Handel. "It's illustrated in the Handel book," he said, but he did not have the book with him and neither did I. When I got the lamp home and did some research, I realized the lamp was not a Handel at all. The signature was a forgery and the shape of the shade was characteristic of the Pittsburgh Lamp, Brass and Glass Company. Because I had a written receipt, I was able to return the lamp and get my money back. That same year I bought a signed Pairpoint lamp from a prominent lamp dealer. When I had it examined under a black light, I discovered it had been repaired. Once again, receipt in hand, I was able to return the lamp.

If you need to return a piece because it has been misrepresented, do so as soon as possible. Any questions you may have about a lamp should be answered within a week. Do not expect that you can use a lamp for several years and then return it because you feel it was improperly described. Some dealers will happily accept back previously purchased pieces for credit while others feel that once it has been sold they never want to see it again. Make certain you discuss return policies with the dealer before you make the purchase.

An antique lamp or fixture is a wonderful enhancement to a home or business. While copies can be made, isn't it nice to own the real thing?

Opposite page: From the 1922-23 Gimbel Brothers "Let There be Light" lamp catalogue.

45. Torchere, a very fine reproduction of early English, finished in soft antique coloring and dull gold. Especially desirable as a pair on console, mantel, or table. Soft comfortable lighting **25.00**

WHEN we think of art, seldom do we associate it with overalls and soiled hands, with machinery and noise, yet who can deny the presence of art in the workshop where are made these lamps of iron?

41. Junior floor lamp of handwrought iron, 63 in. high. Ornamented in gold, Italian blue, wrought iron black or antique ivory. Hand decorated genuine sheep skin parchment 20 in. shade, colored to match. **49.50**

42. Floor torchere with lantern, 72 in. high, of wrought iron in black and gold; flowers and leaves in Italian coloring. Lantern of genuine parchment. Especially attractive at side of doorway, or console table. **42.50**

46. Charming desk or table lamp done in wrought iron finished in soft colorings and dull gold highlights with genuine sheep skin parchment shade. Unusually designed to represent a growing flower. **32.50**

43. Table lamp of wrought iron, 22 in. high, in black, decorated in soft colors, high lighted gold Verd antique marble base. Hand decorated parchment vellum shade. **32.50**

44. Wrought iron reading lamp in black with burnished gold, Italian red and blue decorations. Adjustable arm. Hand decorated genuine sheepskin parchment 12 in. shade. **29.50**

New York : Gimbel Brothers : Philadelphia

Further Information, Resources, and Recommended Reading

I welcome your comments and questions about material published in this book. If you would like to contact me, please write to:

Nadja Maril
Historic Lighting Consultant
Box 6180
Annapolis, Maryland 21401

Resources to Contact for the Further Study of Lighting

The Rushlight Club: Founded in 1932, the purpose of the club is to" stimulate an interest in the study of early lighting including the use of early lighting devices and lighting fluids, and the origins and development of each...." Membership information can be obtained by contacting the Corresponding Secretary, Amanda Sherwin, PO Box 75, Southampton, New York 11969.

Daniel W. Mattaush is a researcher concentrating on the history of gas light and lighting technologies. He can be contacted at Cortelyou House, 260 Maryland NE, Washington, D.C. 20002.

Recommended Reading

Clay, Lancaster. *New York Interiors at the Turn of the Century*. New York: Dover Press, 1976.

Cooke, Lawrence S., Editor. *Lighting in America, From Colonial Rushlights to Victorian Chandeliers*. Pittstown, New Jersey: Main Street Press, 1984.

Courter, J.W., *Aladdin. The Magic Name in Lamps*. Simpson, Illinois: Published by the author, 1971.

Courter, J.W., *Aladdin Electric Lamps*. Simpson, Illinois: Published by the author, 1987.

De Falco, Robert, Carole Goldman Hibbel, and John Hibbel. *Handel Lamps, Painted Shades and Glassware*. Staten Island, New York: H & D Press, 1986.

Denys, Peter Myers. *Gaslighting in America*. New York: Dover Press, 1978.

Duncan, Alistair. *Art Nouveau and Art Deco Lighting*. New York: Simon and Schuster, 1978.

Freeman, Larry. *New Light on Old Lamps*. Watkins Glen, New York: The American Life Foundation, 1968, 1984.

Gledhill, David. *Gas Lighting*. United Kingdom: Shire Publications Ltd., 1981.

Hulebus, Marjorie. *Miniature Victorian Lamps*. Atglen, Pennsylvania: Schiffer Publishing Ltd., 1996.

Malakoff, Edward and Sheila Malakoff. *Pairpoint Lamps*. Atglen, Pennsylvania: Schiffer Publishing Ltd., 1988.

Maril, Nadja. *American Lighting 1840-1940*. Atglen, Pennsylvania: Schiffer Publishing Ltd, 1989,1995.

Meadows, Cecil A. *Discovering Oil Lamps*. United Kingdom: Shire Publications, 1972.

Miller, Richard C. and John E. Solverson. *Student Lamps of the Victorian Era*. Marietta, Ohio: Antique Publications, 1992.

Moss, Roger W. *Lighting for Historic Buildings, A Guide for Selecting Reproductions*. Washington D.C.: The Preservation Press, 1988.

Neudstadt, Dr. Egon. *The Lamps of Tiffany*. New York: The Fairfield Press, 1970.

Roberts, Darrah L. *Collecting Art Nouveau Shades*. Des Moines, Iowa: Wallace-Homestead Book Company, 1972.

Rushlight Club. *Early Lighting, A Pictorial Guide*. Boston, Massachusetts: Compiled and published by the Rushlight Club, 1972.

Smith, Frank R. and Ruth E. Smith. *Miniature Lamps*. Atglen, Pennsylvania: Schiffer Publishing Ltd., 1968.

Smith, Ruth E. *Miniature Lamps II*. Atglen, Pennsylvania: Schiffer Publishing Ltd., 1982.

Thuro, Catherine M.V. *Oil Lamps, The Kerosene Era in North America*. Greensboro, North Carolina: Wallace-Homestead Company, 1976.

Thuro, Catherine M.V. *Oil Lamps II, Glass Kerosene Lamps*. Toronto, Canada: Thorncliffe House, 1983.

Index

Notes